Do It Right

THE

SECOND

TIME

Do It Right

THE

(SECOND)

TIME

Benchmarking Best Practices
in the Quality Change Process

PETER MERRILL

PRODUCTIVITY PRESS
Portland, Oregon

© 1997 by Productivity Press, a division of Productivity, Inc.

Additional copies of this book are available from the publisher. Discounts are available for multiple copies through the Sales Department (800-394-6868). Address all other inquiries to:

Productivity Press
P.O. Box 13390
Portland, OR 97213-0390
United States of America
Telephone: 503-235-0600
Telefax: 503-235-0909
E-mail: service@ppress.com

Book and cover design by William Stanton
Composition by William H. Brunson, Typography Services
Printed and bound by Edwards Brothers in the United States of America

Library of Congress Cataloging-in-Publication Data

Merrill, Peter.
    Do it right the second time : benchmarking best practices in the quality change process / Peter Merrill.
        p.   cm.
    Includes bibliographical references and index.
    ISBN 1-56327-175-3 (hardcover)
    1. Benchmarking (Management)   2. Total quality management.
    I. Title.
    HD62.15.M47   1997
    658.5′62—dc21   97-783
                                                                         CIP

02 01 00 99 98 97 10 9 8 7 6 5 4 3 2 1

To my Parents, Bill and Phyllis Merrill,

for introducing me to the wonderful

journey of life, and to my daughters,

Rachel and Sarah, for reminding me to

stop and smell the roses

Contents

PART III: THE CHANGE

PART IV: THE PROCESSES

PART V: THE PEOPLE

PART VI: THE CONTINUITY

Publisher's Message

Most books on quality tend to catalog glorious triumphs of one company or another, but tell you little about how to handle the failures and pitfalls experienced by nearly every company on the quality path. In *Do It Right the Second Time*, Peter Merrill shares many real-life experiences from his 30 years in management and consulting, not only of successful quality process implementations, but of rebounds from flawed first tries. Above all, believes Merrill, success over the long term is a matter of not giving up when the going gets tough.

Merrill's book is a fascinating odyssey through the uncertain seas of organizational change. On this journey you will meet many fellow travelers whose stories contain valuable lessons about what it means to "do quality" and how to vanquish the challenges that naturally arise in any change process.

Do It Right the Second Time is built around Merrill's model for process improvement, which emphasizes the people side as much as the process itself. Each chapter focuses on an element of the total quality improvement process and enables you to evaluate whether your own quality process has managed that element in a way that would achieve success.

In Part I, Merrill begins by examining the question "Why are we doing this?" Understanding what quality is—and that it's ultimately the *customer's* definition that counts—is the foundation for building, or rebuilding, a quality process that will support your company in the competitive arena of the future.

To have a successful quality process, you must have a vision for what the organization can be, a big picture of what you are all striving for. Parts II and III tell how leaders can develop a vision that articulates and amplifies the values shared in the organization's culture—or in the culture it needs to develop. As Merrill points out, leadership is critical in marshaling people and resources toward a new vision of how the organization can serve its internal and external customers. The quality management team—led by top management—becomes the agent that makes and sustains the transformation into a quality improvement process.

Parts IV and V give the details of the two parts of Merrill's quality improvement model: *process improvement*—process ownership, measurement, cost of quality, and corrective action—and *people improvement*—education, communication, teamwork, and recognition. Part VI deals with systems for continuing the quality process over time. Merrill presents the reorganized 1997 Baldrige Award criteria as a comprehensive system and diagnostic tool for continuous, customer-focused quality improvement. He also underscores the value of ISO 9000 assessment and certification for implementing the process improvement side of quality.

Merrill tells the story of how to do it right the second time in anecdotes and personal tales about what the quality effort has meant in many different organizations. His writing is engaging and colorful, making it pleasant to take this medicine for your quality program. And if you need it in a fast-acting dose, you can catch the basic points in a "Browser's Briefing" review section at the end of each chapter.

If you have not succeeded with your quality program in the first round, read this book. Identify mistakes you may have made and learn how to correct them. If you are just starting, use Merrill's lessons to avoid the pitfalls made by others.

We'd like to acknowledge the many people who helped produce this book. First, of course, thanks to Peter Merrill for selecting Productivity Press as publisher. Thanks also to Valerie Braun of Strider International for assistance in assembling the manuscript. At Productivity Press, thanks to Steven Ott, president, and Diane Asay, editor in chief, for their support of the project; to Mary Junewick, Karen Jones, and Susan Swanson for editorial and prepress management; and to Bill Stanton for design. Special thanks to Bill Brunson for typography and page makeup, and to Marvin Moore for proofreading.

Norman Bodek
Publisher

Preface

In the early part of the twentieth century, my grandfather taught chemistry at Batley Grammar School in Yorkshire, England. This was the same school attended during the eighteenth century by Joseph Priestley, the father of modern chemistry. Like many of his contemporaries, Herbert Merrill came out of World War I a changed man. He entered the Congregational church. He became a Minister of Religion.

In the 1920s, Herbert Merrill's elder son, William, was a student at Batley Grammar School. Bill Merrill also rejected the world of chemistry and in the 1930s became an engineer in the brave new world of electrical engineering. However, he didn't turn his back on the church. He became a Methodist lay preacher, serving the church in that role for his entire life.

I was born in the latter years of World War II in the industrial heartland of Britain, which experienced so much devastation during that war. In the 1950s, as I progressed through King Edward VI School in Aston, Birmingham, I didn't realize the strong influence these two men had already exerted on my life. For some reason, I found chemistry incredibly exciting and continually excelled in the subject. However, I started to feel there was something beyond chemistry and discovered chemical engineering. I read chemical engineering at Birmingham University, and although it was alleged to be the best chemical engineering school in the country, the lecturers and professors there played little direct part in my acquiring knowledge in the subject. I acquired a degree in tenacity, as well as a degree in chemical engineering.

I left Birmingham, having ingrained myself with the principles of process management, little knowing that 25 years later those skills would become an integral part of my understanding of the art and science of quality management.

My grandmother, Edith Merrill, taught at a small village school in Yorkshire. I always had the desire to be a teacher or a preacher, but my experience at Birmingham University had drawn me away from joining such a body of people. My mother, Phyllis Merrill, taught me the basics in life: conformance to requirements, a stitch in time saves nine, and always look for a better way of doing things. She gave me the basic set of values that are fundamental to making quality a way of life.

Many years later, when I was going through a period of huge turmoil, I met a passionate Welsh mystic named James Angove. In one of our conversations, I jokingly commented that my family had progressed downward from Grandfather being a full-time minister of the church to my father a part-time minister of the church, to myself who although I held strong beliefs, now rarely if ever attended a church. I had become a full-time practitioner of quality management. "On the contrary," James replied. "You are a Minister of Business."

My career after Birmingham University led me into a large British corporation, Courtaulds, and chemical engineering enabled me to work in the United States, South Africa, and Scandinavia. Far more personal growth was open to me than doing postgraduate research in "Catalytic Distillation Involving the Use of Cuprammonium Salts," the Ph.D. subject I had been offered. From 1969 till 1987, my career with Courtaulds then took me away from the soulless world of chemical engineering into the very exciting people-oriented world of textiles with all its passions, emotions, and ethnic influences. In fact, within eight years of graduating as a chemical engineer, I left Courtaulds for a time and become a fashion designer. My old professor would have turned in his grave.

Three years later, in 1976, I rejoined Courtaulds, having graduated through the "University of Life," being ripped off by professional crooks called retailers, having operated my own market stall, and wondering if a check would come tomorrow to cover the food I bought yesterday. I then progressed along a marketing route to become involved for over a decade with Christy, one of Britain's best known household brands.

William Miller Christy invented the humble product we have come to know as the "towel," and nearly 150 years later, Christy towels are still recognized as a quality product.

It was during the early 1980s that I first encountered people talking about quality as if it was a great new religion for the business world. Roger Milliken, in conversation with Alan Nightingale, the then chairman of the Courtauld Textiles Group, had sparked interest in this "new" approach to running a business; Milliken later became world famous as one of the great champions of quality management. I was by then chief executive of one of the businesses in Courtaulds, and my biggest customer was Marks and Spencer, the world's most successful retailer. They said to me, "In five year's time, all of our suppliers will need to be involved in a quality improvement process." Familiar words?

Between 1984 and 1987, as chief executive of this business with the Courtaulds Group, I experienced the obstacles that you yourself may have experienced in trying to make quality a way of life.

In 1987 I was given an opportunity most people in the world of quality would envy and worked for the next four years with one of the great gurus of quality. Philip Crosby enabled me to immerse in a world of both "thinking and doing" quality which I would have found nowhere else. I worked with Crosby initially in the United States and later in Canada. I moved on from working with him shortly after he "retired" in 1991. But I am still grateful for the insights and thought processes he initiated.

In 1991, I became involved in the American Society for Quality Control (ASQC) in Canada, and in 1994 was honored to become chair of the Toronto section, one of the largest in North America. The friendships and growth in knowledge that have come from the ASQC are something for which I will be eternally grateful.

Since 1987, I have worked with nearly a hundred different chief executives around the world who have experienced the same problems you have. "We did all the education, then it died." "We never did get to using cost of quality." "We have created a wonderful culture, but can't see any evidence of improvement on the bottom line." "We could never work out what to measure, so we're not sure if improvement happened."

In the chapters ahead, I will show you how many companies going through the same experiences as you found the right way to make quality happen after often trying the wrong way. *They did it right the second time.*

ACKNOWLEDGMENTS

I want to thank the people in the world of quality who gave their time and gave me such special feedback from the original manuscript: John Varley, from Quest Management Services; Jim Clemmer, author of *Firing on All Cylinders;* Barry Goode, Quality Director at IBM; Russ Wharton, of Wharton Associates; Arnold Gedmintas, of Cadet Uniform Services; Don Irwin; Brian Sayer, of Nacan Products; John McDonald, author of *Global Quality;* Philip Crosby, author of *Quality Is Free.*

A deep debt is owed to Tony Hightower, who pulled together scribblings faxed to him from all over the world and made the original manuscript a legible document.

Introduction

Many organizations are looking back on the quality initiative they pursued at some time in the last ten years and saying, "It failed." Others are quietly walking away and letting quality die a silent death. Failure rates as high as 70 percent are being quoted. However, more than a few people are saying quality is the best thing that ever happened to them and they wouldn't be around today without their quality process.

Looking at these successes, we find they *also* had failure. They learned from their failure, though, and moved on to do it right the second time. Looking at the successful quality processes enables us to see where and how we can improve our own quality improvement process. You could call it "benchmarking" other quality processes, or to quote C.S. Wallace, Jr., of the Baldrige-winning Wallace Company of Texas, "Some people call it benchmarking. I call it 'kinda copyin.'"

More than anything else, the successful companies never gave up, and they found that regular "self-assessment" of their quality activity was essential. They have defined the quality process they have been through and have taken time to measure and understand their quality process. Their quality process had a plan and a structure, and they applied the principles of continuous improvement to the quality process itself.

Successful quality systems show these common factors:

- The people in the organization all know why they are involved in quality and where they are heading. They have a clear vision.

• The change to the new vision was initiated by the leadership of the organization but the change activity has then been shared with everyone in the organization.

• The change process has clearly defined subprocesses or components and there is a balance between people improvement and process improvement.

• The performance of the quality process is measured continuously in order to drive improvement of that quality process and there is built-in continuity in the change process.

The people who did not "do it right the first time" failed to implement at least one of these four elements in their quality improvement strategy. In this book we'll look in turn at each of these aspects of quality processes, and see how some very ordinary people made extraordinary changes in their own lives and the lives of the people around them. They learned from their mistakes. They are people like you and me, and we can all learn from their experiences, to do it right the second time.

If you want to become a quality organization, you must first know what one looks like. Nowadays, there are plenty of them around, but you can't just simply copy other people. You have to build your own vision and use the best parts of other people's ideas.

Nearly 20 years ago, a young mountaineer named Quentin Wahl was starting a small business in the dry cleaning industry. He had learned a lot about the industry when he was a student. He was staggered at the amount of rework and customer dissatisfaction that occurred because people didn't do it right the first time. This wasn't the fault of the people; they wanted to do a good job. Quentin built a picture in his mind of a company in the industry in which people did it right the first time. His vision wasn't just kept to himself. He found a partner for his journey into quality and customer service. Arnold Gedmintas became the "doer," and Quentin Wahl the "thinker," as they built Cadet Uniform Services, a company that developed over 99 percent customer retention and became a finalist in the Canadian Award for Business Excellence.

Do you know why your business exists? Is it to make money, and little else? Or is it a venture people will remember for its mark on the world?

As we look deeper into these visions, we also see organizations that have firm principles or values on which the vision is built. Successful organizations in quality have clear quality values that are practiced by everyone in the organization. Thomas Watson, Sr., gave IBM its Basic Beliefs of "respect for the individual, best possible service to our customer, and every task performed in a superior manner." Before joining Cadet, prospective employees are asked to study overnight the principles of quality that the company supports, and they are given a long and rigorous interview process to ensure they have the same value system as the other people in the organization.

The values are what create the culture of the organization. Believing in such basic principles as conformance to customer requirements, delivering quality through prevention, and continuous improvement are the foundation stones of a quality culture.

Philip Crosby published his book *Quality Is Free* in 1979. His "overnight success" was actually the result of more than 20 years of hard work. He left ITT and set up his consulting practice. Although he was not seeking to build a large organization, the customer was hungry for Crosby's knowledge, and his organization for delivering this knowledge grew with each customer request. Crosby had a vision of an organization serving as a role model of "quality culture" to the world. He succeeded in that mission, and created a company of some 300 people where relationships were based on trust and respect, and knowledge was shared for the greater good of the team, not hoarded as a way to leverage power. People in the company would work at an unbelievable rate because of their passionate belief in the organization and the set of values on which it had been founded.

It is easy to assume that everyone has the same values or beliefs we do. But value systems differ between individuals, between families, between companies, and between nations. Successful organizations in quality have established a set of quality values at the outset, and a big part of the success of the Crosby approach in the 1980s was Philip Crosby's Four Absolutes, which are a basic set of quality values.

Quality values are the foundation for the quality culture of any organization.

The whole move to a "quality organization" involves change. Most of us like variation and change, but few of us like *being* changed. The successful quality organizations have built in the desire to change. The leaders want change and are visibly giving up old practices. They see the power in working as a leadership team to make change happen. The team understands its role as a primary agent for change. It is not a corrective action team. It is a team that plans the change process, but as individuals the team members participate in the change activities inside the organization. Above all, they are a role model for change.

Joseph Juran said, many years ago, "You plan and implement quality in the same way you plan and implement your finances."

Leadership and leadership commitment are repeatedly cited as the cause of success or failure in a quality process, and yet everyone has a leadership role to play. Ontario Hydro's general manager in Pickering, after two years in a quality process, found that his greatest need was more training in leadership. He trains every new team leader in leadership skills before placing that person on their project. This is common sense when you think about it, and yet we always want to get on with the job instead of developing skills first.

Our perception of a good leader has become more "educated." We now see ourselves seeking a leader who listens and is honest, rather than one who "motivates" and "orders." The Malcolm Baldrige National Quality Award criteria, for example, look for how the company's leadership "incorporates clear values, company directions, high performance expectations, a strong customer focus, and continuous learning" (1997 Baldrige Award Criteria).

The change to a quality and customer service organization requires a change process, and many overlook this truth. The simplest truth about change is that it is continuous, and you must either change or face the fate of the dinosaurs. The second truth is that change must be led; but remember, people will not *be* changed. Change has to ultimately be shared with everyone in your organization. Most people accept these truths intellectually, but not always emotionally. The third truth about changing to a quality organization is that there must be a balance between people improvement and process improvement. Too many organizations focus on one or the other and don't keep that balance. You need the process analysis, measurement, and cost of quality, but they must be balanced with education, development of communication skills, and recognition of people's improvements.

This need for balance between people and process was seen over 60 years ago by W. Edwards Deming, when he worked with Elton Mayo (soft skills) and Walter Shewhart (hard skills). People are talking today as if it is a new revelation. Let's give credit where it is due!

We see some interesting lessons on people and process improvement from organizations that have succeeded in continuous improvement. This book will share some of their stories to learn from.

PROCESS IMPROVEMENTS

On the process side of quality, *process ownership* is the critical but often overlooked foundation work for process management. The Scarborough branch of Employment Canada, the process owners mapped their process and streamlined it to reduce cycle time and serve their clients faster. The people in the office know who their internal customers and suppliers are, and have invested time and effort in defining the requirements of their customers. This work has enabled the employees to focus on the requirements where problems exist, and to move to the next stage of process improvement: *measurement.*

Bart DiLiddo, the former CEO of B.F. Goodrich, was asked to name the most critical success factor in his quality process. He responded without hesitation: "Meaningful measurement." Measurement doesn't have to be technical or complicated, but it does have to be meaningful to the customer. In a successful organization, measurement involves everyone, not just the technical people. The measurement data is used to find the root cause of problems, and to measure the effectiveness of their solutions.

The third element of process improvement, *cost of quality,* is one of the most powerful tools in your quality toolbox. It is widely misunderstood and is the subject of great controversy. One division of telecommunications specialist Mitel used cost of quality to drive its corrective action system and understood how cost of quality is really a medium for translating your wealth of measurement data into the dollar language of business. David Rayfield, the managing director, was proud of how cost of quality had saved millions, and enabled management to select their corrective action projects on a dispassionate return on investment basis instead of the more usual "whim of the moment." A major international food company carrying out a "first cut" on cost of quality discovered that its annual budgeting process was one of the biggest cost wastes, losing half a million dollars a year simply because the process and its requirements had not been clearly defined and communicated. What a great incentive for process improvement!

Cost of quality is the link between measurement and *corrective action*. As I've learned from personal experience, it's important to set the scope for action on the front side; otherwise the program may be discredited when the actions proposed are too expensive or otherwise undoable.

The corrective action system should be launched companywide only after establishing process ownership, measurement, and a cost of quality system. Cost of quality is then used to prioritize the projects you will take on, and people will discover that capital projects are not where the big opportunities exist. It's interpersonal communications and operating procedures where the biggest improvements are often needed.

PEOPLE IMPROVEMENTS

All too often organizations focus on the tangible process improvement areas and forget the "people improvement." People improvement is the "right brain" part of the change model.

The first activity in people improvement is *education*. Most organizations who have worked on quality have realized the importance of the educational investment, and yet many have invested wholesale and without a real plan. Our common perception of education is that it should be done in huge chunks. This is partly because of the "school" paradigm we all carry, and partly because we find education a nuisance and a disruption to our daily routine, so we try to get it over with quickly. The other side of the coin is being trapped in education. Successful companies have avoided these problems by using "just-in-time" education.

An education specialist named Treat Hull (a hard name to forget) said, "The half-life of education is about 30 days. In other words, unless you use it, you lose it!" These companies all followed the "learn a bit, do a bit" approach—probably 1½ to 2½ hours each week in which people acquired skills or tools to be used in the upcoming week. The "action assignment" during the week is critical, linking each of the education sessions to the real world. It takes a lot more organizing, but it's infinitely more effective.

One effect of your education will be that people talk to each other far more than they did in the past. Poor *communication* is the biggest obstacle most people cite as stopping their company from delivering quality. Communication has to be improved at an interpersonal level as well as at the organizational level. Developing interpersonal communication skills is a very long-term process, and needs to be built in to all the other education, teamwork, and process management work you carry out. The company communication systems can be developed far more quickly. Chapter 15 describes the team briefing method pioneered by an organization called the Industrial Society, which used the technique to overcome major communication barriers typical of British companies, where the old class structure and schooling structure has thwarted communication for decades.

Better communication is a foundation for improved *teamwork*. Building a "team" is one of the popular views of what quality is all about. It is an important component, but it is only a component. If you have worked on "team performance," "team building," or "teamwork," you know that these are only a part of the quality jigsaw. They have not given you "quality." Similarly, if you have worked on measurement or reengineering or problem solving you have only worked on part of the quality process.

John Billing, the director of human resources at Courtaulds, saw the importance of this teamwork component in an organization that had a high technical and product focus. A challenging whitewater rafting expedition on the Chattooga River created a bond between the managers in that organization that would be hard to break. Different nations have differing aptitudes for teamwork. Your organization must have a high teamwork aptitude if it is going to succeed in quality. It means trusting and respecting each other.

Recognition of effort and accomplishment is critical along the way. As you go through these changes, people will feel insecure. The simple act of saying thank you to each person who does something the "new way" is a critical factor in reinforcing new behaviors based on your new values.

Bell Cellular (now Bell Mobility) developed a recognition system that was one of the most exciting you could come across. This was due in large part to company president Bob Latham's passionate belief in recognition. He also provided everyone with tools for recognition so that it became easy for a person to thank someone else who did a good job or who helped you do a good job.

CONTINUATION OF IMPROVEMENT

Building continuity into your quality process is a tough challenge, and one of the best ways of maintaining ongoing improvement in your quality process is by measuring or evaluating its effectiveness.

Baldrige Award criteria assessment has proved one of the most complete methods so far for evaluating an organization's quality plan. It is comprehensive, though many have found it cumbersome. Describing in writing the activities inside an organization has become too time-consuming for most companies. This has led to a number of simplified versions of the Baldrige criteria that enable companies to conduct a self-assessment on their quality process.

Of the 1,000-point scale used in a Baldrige assessment, a reactive organization will score up to 400 points. The majority of quality conscious companies score between 400 and 600 points. Above this band we find the aspiring world class companies who are developing their own quality processes and benchmarking against best of breed with relative ease. It is the "new kids on the block" with scores below 300 who have the difficulties, and many of them have seized on ISO 9000 to solve their problem. ISO does not directly enable a company to measure the effectiveness of its quality process but it does provide an excellent foundation for beginning the process. ISO gives discipline to the operation of an organization and enables it to find out from an independent third party "how well are we doing?"

Many organizations, such as Sears, have adapted the ISO requirements and applied a score system to the audit checklist. Sears uses this to assess their suppliers as well as themselves. Howard Tremaine manages the Sears Supplier Quality Partnership, and he and his team give each Sears supplier a percentage score. This score gives the supplier an idea of overall performance, enabling it to focus on the areas of the business needing improvement.

The "thinking-learning" organizations then use this information to look back at their quality improvement process and find whether they need to improve measurement, communication, or some other aspect of the quality process.

The other reason quality "beginners" are turning to ISO is that it enables them to lay those foundation stones of process ownership and education, while the more quality-mature organizations are using ISO to go back and fill in the missing parts of the foundation. This can be dangerous thinking for beginners, however, because ISO does not fully address the soft skill side of quality. Some companies think when they've got ISO 9000, they've got quality. More and more companies are now seeing the need to build in the teamwork, communication, and recognition activities that are needed to balance the process improvement.

Whether it is Baldrige, ISO 9000, or some other method of assessing the organization, companies that use the assessment feedback to improve their business processes can also use the information to improve their quality improvement process by identifying which parts of the improvement process need to be strengthened.

We now see the continuous nature of this journey—which brings me back to my opening remark: More than anything else, the successful companies never gave up.

PART I

THE REASON

1 | Why Are We Doing This?

There has to be a reason...

The town of Salisbury in the county of Wiltshire in the kingdom of England was the scene of enormous activity between the years of 1220 and 1365, before Shakespeare wrote his plays and before Columbus sailed the seas. Among many other activities, you would have seen stonemasons cutting huge rocks into blocks which were as much as eighteen inches thick by two feet long by a foot high. These blocks weighed a quarter of a ton apiece.

A troupe of strolling players entered Salisbury one summer, and seeing the activity, one of the troubadours approached a mason and asked him, "What art thou doing?" The mason gave a bored look and replied, "I am cutting these stones into blocks."

"But why in the world wouldst thou do such a thing?" questioned the troubadour.

The mason replied, "Because I need the money they pay me for this."

The troubadour was disappointed at the fast response he received, and rejoined the group of players. However, a few minutes further down the road, the troubadour saw another stonemason who looked far more enthusiastic than the previous mason. Still curious and without hesitation, he made a second approach. "I see so many of you cutting the stone; prithee, what is your task?"

The mason looked up and without hesitation replied, "I am part of the team that is helping to build this great cathedral!" The troubadour felt the emotion and excitement and he danced with glee, for he had realized that he was witness to one of the great events in the history of humanity.

Are the people in your organization cutting stone, or are they building a cathedral?

Do you know why your business exists? Is it to make money and little else? Or is it a venture people will remember for its mark on the world, in the same way as Salisbury Cathedral, a magnificent creation which still stands 600 years later, in all its glory?

How do you want your organization to be remembered in the community and in the world? Is your organization going to be remembered as a great cathedral in the community, or just as a wooden shack which survived four or five years, and then collapsed and rotted away?

BEING SUCCESSFUL

Do you want to be successful?

A stupid question? Perhaps. What do we mean by success? What does it look like? What does it feel like?

Is it winning the lottery? Is it having lots of money? Long weekends on tropical islands, or owning a private jet? For a lot of people, success really means escaping from where they feel trapped at the moment.

Real, lasting success comes when we enjoy doing what we do every day and when we do it well.

I once picked up a fortune cookie note that said, "Success comes from hard work." True up to a point, but the word *hard* implies unpleasant, painful work. I want to enjoy my work.

I passed that note to my daughter just before her high school finals, as a great reminder of the importance of hard work and also because I'd come by another fortune cookie note that said, "The secret of a good opportunity is recognizing it!" The implication is clear. We need to have clear focus and application in our efforts (hard work), but we must also be sure that our efforts are pointed in the right direction (a clear vision).

So success in our business endeavors means doing what we do better than the competition does it, and ensuring our customers recognize that we do a good job.

HOW DO WE BECOME SUCCESSFUL?

If you want success and an organization in which you will have long-term pride, then you have probably tried some type of quality improvement activity in the last few years.

If you have, then you probably also know that you are in the majority if your improvement activity has not yet succeeded. But you tried a quality program because you wanted to be more successful.

Having asked yourself, "Why are we involved in quality?" perhaps you should also ask, "*What* are we doing?"

- Total Quality Management

- Quality Improvement

- Continuous Process Improvement

- Business Process Reengineering

- ISO 9000

- Or perhaps Kaizen?

Or are you actually in the process of renaming your failure as you read this book? This is like saying your child has been so obnoxious during the terrible twos that you will change their name from Bobby to Billy, or from Karen to Christine, on their third birthday. Changing the name is not going to change your chance of success.

This brings you back to the question, *"Why are we doing this?"*; and if your company is asking "Why?" about its quality process, then you need to go right back to the beginning, and ask yourselves, "Did we ever ask that question in the first place?" You probably did, and you probably got many different answers:

- Survival

- The customer

- Increased market share
- More profit
- To get ISO 9000 certification
- To improve the culture
- To reduce waste

Did you then take the time to link all those answers together so that everyone in the organization understood how those answers relate? All the answers boil down to making your company more successful.

THE CUSTOMER DECIDES

The customer ultimately decides whether your company will be successful or not.

Have you dealt with a customer complaint in the last seven days? If you did, you probably didn't enjoy the experience, although you may have gotten some satisfaction if you resolved the complaint and made the customer happy. This customer opinion of our products and services is the most valuable driving force for our business—it makes us focus on opportunities for improvement.

Do you know why your customers switch to other suppliers? The big picture is surprising:

- 50 percent leave due to poor service.
- 20 percent leave due to lack of personal contact.
- 15 percent leave due to inferior product.
- 15 percent leave because the product is too expensive.

Your own company may be different, but this data gives us some food for thought. Most companies don't realize they are a blend of both manufacturing and service. We think of McDonald's as a service organization, and yet we all know they have a factory out back that makes the food we eat. We may be manufacturing chemicals, but the bigger issue we probably face with our customers is much more likely to be the quality of our service than the quality of our product.

If we are going to be competitive in the marketplace, we have to offer both top quality product and top quality service, and the two are inextricably linked.

Successful companies are talking to their customers all the time. One of my clients, Cadet Uniform Services, which has a 99.4 percent customer retention rate, employs 300 people in its operation and conducts 3,500 customer interviews every year. You have to go and talk to the customer.

The more senior we get in the organization, the more reluctant we become. I remember once, when I was working as a sales manager, my secretary received what I knew would be a serious customer complaint call. I asked my assistant Chris Armstead to take the call. Chris and I were good friends, and he made a telling remark back to me: "Send in the infantry to clear the way for the cavalry!" Too many leaders are not prepared to hear it straight from the customer, and too many customers are also not prepared to tell it straight to the business leaders. The customer doesn't want to jeopardize people inside your organization. Customers complain like this:

- 5 percent complain to the top.
- 45 percent complain to the representative.
- 50 percent complain to our potential customers.

When I say our potential customer, that can be our customer's competitor, but it is more likely to be our customer's customer. How often do you hear a sales assistant say to you, "Yes, this product is unreliable," or "I don't know when we'll get our next delivery?" Your performance is being communicated in the marketplace every day, even as we speak.

So why don't we get involved in these customer complaints? The tension, abuse, and the wasted time away from creative work are all good reasons. But quality is about delivering products and service that delight the customer and being better at it than the competition, and it has to be led from the top of the organization.

The reasons for customer problems vary from one organization to another. During the 1970s and 1980s in large organizations such as IBM and General Motors, both the leaders and the employees lost touch with the customer. On the other hand, many smaller organizations who prided themselves on customer responsiveness didn't realize the internal chaos and waste they created in being responsive to one customer while jeopardizing the service they gave to another customer.

HOW SHOULD WE USE THIS KNOWLEDGE?

Even with good data on how we satisfy the customer, what do we do with it? There is a strange paradox here. People with technical backgrounds and who are reputedly left-brain (or analytical) in their approach frequently react by using right-brain, or creative, solutions. What I mean by this is that we seek some innovative product improvement, in the hope that it will make the customer forgive and forget the appalling service we have been giving them. I speak from firsthand experience. My business used to supply Marks and Spencer's, England's well-known retailer. We continually flooded them with product innovations as we tried to hang on to them as customers. They, in turn, were increasingly frustrated with our failure to deliver complete, on-time orders and so were constantly trying to develop alternative suppliers.

We should focus our strong analytical powers on our customer data and direct those wonderful creative energies to improving the service aspects of quality.

There are some wonderful examples of this blend of analytical and creative problem solving which excite my imagination. Edward de Bono, in his book *Sur Petition*, talks of how a brainstorming session with Ford Motor Company executives in England unearthed the biggest hassle that Ford drivers experienced. It was not the car they drove, but finding a parking space. He made the crazy suggestion that Ford should buy a chain of parking lots which would be available only to Ford owners. I can tell you if I drove in London, that would be a major attraction for me to buy a Ford. In the United States, State Farm Insurance is working with IBM to develop a chip that State Farm automobile drivers can install in their vehicle to, in the event of an accident, notify the nearest State Farm office of the vehicle, the owner, and the location. The State Farm agent would arrive at the accident scene at the same time as the police and deal with all the issues that would worry the motorist, including finding a replacement vehicle.

What are the issues that you should be tackling to delight your customer? What are the aspects of your product or service that really cause them grief?

We talk about The Customer; who is this strange person? It's actually a many-headed monster, like the mythological Hydra! You may have as many as twenty different interfaces, or "moments of truth," with your "customer." Their purchasing clerk, the buyer, the president, the R&D staff, the accounts payable office, and the receiving bay. Where I've mentioned a department, there may be several people who can each be a customer. Shipping the product is only one part of the story. You need to ship the related information in an accurate, timely, and user-friendly manner as well.

Often customers do not get what they want because of unnecessary internal wasted time and wasted cost, or because customers' requirements on price, reliability, or service are simply not met. Unhappy customers mean a less successful business.

WHAT STOPS US FROM SUCCEEDING?

The arguments start when we try to agree on how we will become more successful, and who and what will make us more successful. During more than ten years of helping different organizations to be successful in delivering quality to their customers, these ten main obstacles (or should we say opportunities) to delivery have emerged:

1. Poor communication

2. Unclear and changing requirements

3. Lack of senior management commitment

4. Employee cynicism and poor morale

5. Lack of training

6. Bad suppliers

7. Not sticking to procedures

8. Quick fixes

9. Lack of time

10. Lack of process ownership

These are in no special order, and will differ in priority between companies. It is worth mentioning, though, that poor communication usually comes at the top of the list. However, they all lead to wasted time and wasted cost that get in the way of success.

Any form of internal waste means you're asking the customer to pay for something they don't want, and that *you* are paying for something *you* don't want.

"SO HOW MUCH DO WE WASTE?"

I've worked with nearly a hundred different organizations in Europe and North America, helping them calculate how much they waste by not doing it right the first time. In nearly every case, these companies have found *over a million dollars of waste* for every ten million they spend in doing business. I stress that *they* have found this opportunity; I have only shown them how. These organizations have also insisted that the figure they uncovered at the end of one day of assessment probably represents only one-third to one-half of the opportunity for improving their business. To put it another way, your organization is probably wasting one-quarter to one-third of its operating costs by not doing it right the first time. So either your customer is paying too much for your goods and services, or you are working long hours for a very poor reward.

Most businesses who entered a quality improvement process in the last decade have not taken the trouble to calculate their opportunity, or didn't know how. You can do it very easily, if you take the right approach.

Remember, the reason why you are "doing quality" is to make you a more successful organization by serving your customer in a better way.

However, your approach has to be very different from those brutal cost-cutting blitzes we endured in the 1970s and in the early 1990s.

Quality improvement is partly a "business diet," but mainly a change in lifestyle. You want to change that surplus fat into muscle, just as an athlete would during the preseason training for any sport. Athletes notice that training often causes them to gain weight as they build muscle. Quality improvement should change your organization's fat into customer-focused muscle, and turn you into an athletic organization whose limbs are well coordinated and ready to respond. Being athletic does not necessarily mean losing weight.

Those cost reduction programs of the early seventies (and the early nineties) often severed organizational limbs in crisis surgery, in an attempt to lose weight. When this crippled organization, missing critical parts, tried to respond to the customer, its survival only became more threatened.

HOW DO WE FIND THIS WASTE?

When you want to improve your fitness, you need a diagnosis that tells you where your weaknesses are located. Your body will speak for itself. Often we assume that the organizational leaders are the brain which knows all that is happening internally. You need to involve everyone in this diagnosis.

The best way to find out where your organizational waste exists is to ask people. You'll be amazed at the frankness of many answers, and you'll be amazed when people start to quantify those answers. Use a "first cut" cost of quality (described in Chapter 12) to identify where your improvement opportunities exist, and be sure to have it facilitated by someone who understands quality and cost of quality. Don't try to find this number in your financial records; you'll probably only find between 2 percent and 3 percent of your operating costs (a little more if you use activity-based costing). This first cut is a one- or a two-day task that touches each of your managers at some point in that time, and will unearth between a third and one-half of your total cost of waste.

It is vital that you calculate this number yourselves, in order to truly believe the opportunities that lie ahead. However, you should use someone who truly understands cost of quality to facilitate the activity, or you won't open all your options, and, more importantly, you'll never get to the end of the job.

The end result must be a number that is owned by the people who calculated it, so they then have a great desire to get started in quality improvement. One of the big surprises will be that your greatest cost of waste is not in your operations area, but in the finance, or sales, or planning functions. I remember working with a major international food company, where we did a first cut in the finance division alone. Their operating costs were about $4 million, and we unearthed $500,000 wasted in that division by not doing it right the first time.

Do you know what the biggest villain was? The annual budget! The reason: unclear requirements!

How many times a year do you rebudget? Be honest: two, three, four times? Be honest again: are the requirements clear, and do people observe them? Is the time needed to prepare the budget properly planned?

This assessment will give you issues to tackle at both the business level and the department level. You may find issues like labor turnover, absenteeism, or overdue accounts at the business level, or budget preparation, the photocopier, or invoicing errors at the department level. Either way, if you do the job properly, you will give yourself a "significant emotional experience," and cause yourself to want to change the way you do business.

You may also choose at this point to assess your business at a more strategic level, using the Baldrige criteria, and at a more operational level, with an ISO 9000 audit.

At a strategic level, the Baldrige Award assessment process is probably the most rigorous assessment method available. However, be warned that if you have no quality improvement plan, the findings will cause a severe dent in your company ego.

These assessments will answer the question, "Why should I be doing quality?" All of these waste items are getting in the way of your success.

They are getting in the way of your delivering what you promised to your customer.

HOW DO WE ELIMINATE THIS WASTE?

I must warn you against rushing off to tackle what *appear* to be the problems of your business by firing your guns in all directions. It took you a long time to get into this situation, and it will take you some time to get out of it. More importantly, you need to tackle the underlying causes that allowed these situations to develop.

The first cut cost of quality is described in more detail in Chapter 12. It will get your people involved, and will ask them to contribute their ideas. You should follow up with a detailed assessment of where all people in the organization see the need for improvement. Now that their minds have been unlocked, capture their thoughts.

So you need to be very clear at the outset why you are involved in improving your organization. Assessment of your organization for the cost, organizational, and customer benefits will tell you at the outset where improvements are needed and how big your opportunity is.

That brings us back to the fundamental reason any organization exists, and that is to successfully deliver a product or service to the customer.

Incidentally, Salisbury Cathedral is a service organization that has successfully delivered pleasure, inspiration, and comfort to millions of people for centuries.

You need a process which is going to change your organization into the place you want it to be. The change must be customer-driven, which means listening to and understanding what your customer wants. The change must be aimed at a clear target, which means having a clear vision of what you want your new organization to look like. The bad news for some is that this change will never stop. Both our processes and our people must be continuously improving if we are to be successful in an ever-changing world.

In Chapter 2 we'll look more closely at where to focus all this activity. The customer has to be the focus of the success we want our organization to achieve.

- You must define success in terms that pertain to more than just "profit."
- The customer is the final arbiter on whether you deliver quality service and quality products.
- The customer is the final arbiter on whether you will succeed.
- Quality and success are synonymous.
- Don't rename your quality process to be fashionable.
- Do focus on specific aspects of your quality process when the foundations are in place.
- Customers will not tell you where you are failing unless you ask persistently.
- The customer is a many-headed Hydra.
- There is a paradox whereby left-brain people use right-brain methods (and vice versa) to solve customer problems. This is a weakness of the "quick fix."
- There are many obstacles to your success. Communication, commitment, and cynicism are only a few.
- A cost of quality assessment will identify the weaknesses inside your business and make you approach improvement in a planned manner.
- A cost of quality assessment will energize your people and commit your leadership.
- You must build a strategic quality improvement plan which is analogous to your business plan, and the customer must be the driving force.
- You must develop a clear picture (or vision) of where you are heading, and share this with everyone in the organization.
- You must be clear on what you want your organization to be like in two, three, and five years from now.

2 | The Customer

The reason your business exists…

The Maistrali restaurant is in the town of Rethymnon on the north coast of the Greek island of Crete. The owner is Vasilis Pantalos; he knows who the customer is, and he knows that his customer drives the business. Vasilis stands at the front of his restaurant and is the first person to meet his customers when they walk in.

My daughters, Rachel and Sarah, and I were taking a vacation in Crete, and had the good fortune to walk into the Maistrali. Vasilis told us about his restaurant and about the food that he served. He told us about the musicians that played. He wasn't pushy or aggressive, but he clearly believed in his restaurant and knew how it operated. Vasilis also knew his customers, and knew that they were tired of the other restaurants in town where hired hawkers (the locals call them "hooks") stood outside, trying to fast-talk unsuspecting tourists into establishments with less than average food delivered with less than average service.

We had a wonderful time at the Maistrali because Vasilis had also created an environment of relaxed enjoyment in his restaurant. Amazingly, it was the only restaurant in town that played the wonderful Sirtaki music that is everyone's lasting memory of Greece.

The other thing that was significant as we walked into the restaurant was that the local people were eating there, and the unexpected bonus at the end of the evening was the dancing, which my daughters loved to join in.

Vasilis was the leader of that organization. He was in contact with his customer, and he ensured that the inside of his organization had the ability to deliver what the customer wanted. Needless to say, we revisited the Maistrali, and recommend it to other visitors to Crete.

LEADERS MUST TALK TO THE CUSTOMER

Most other organizations start this way, but with time, many leaders hand over the customer contact to the fast-talking "hooks" who try to manipulate the unsuspecting customer. Once the contract is signed, the hooks lose all further interest in the client until the time comes for a repeat order, and the "salesman" starts to make promises. Or the organization makes promises to the salesman, and everyone gets angry because the customer didn't get what was promised last time.

The transition from customer contact by the business leader to customer contact by other persons in the organization was a critical point in the history of your organization. It often happens imperceptibly, because the moment you have more than one interface with the customer, then you have transactions in which the business leader is not a participant.

It's not just the salesperson who takes away customer contact from the leader; it's also the accounts receivable clerk, the dispatch manager, the research and development staff, the delivery driver…

WHO IS THE CUSTOMER?
WHAT DOES THE CUSTOMER WANT?

I recall conducting a strategic planning session with LePage Adhesives, a household brand, and helping them identify nearly 20 different points of contact with the customer. Each of these "moments of truth" affects the reputation of your organization with the customer.

IBM went through great trauma as their business shrank in 1992. To their credit, they put tremendous effort into asking the customer what were the major barriers to conducting business with IBM. One of the most widespread problems turned out to be the invoice system. Little things, like "Big Blue" using blue ink on its forms, which would not then reproduce on the client's photocopier. As IBM staff dug deeper into the problem and implemented customer-friendly solutions, they witnessed a dramatic drop in credit notes and an increase in customer satisfaction.

American Express was very proud of the speed with which it issues a card to a new customer, but wondered why its business shrank in favor of Visa. In the 1990s, Amex customers continued to be angry with statements that were a maze of irrelevant code, and which did not carry dates against the transactions. I canceled my membership after the frustrating failure of their internal communications and repeated unfriendly contacts with their customer service staff. Since then they have discovered what their customers wanted and have updated the format of their statement.

Smart sales tricks will not hold your customers if you are repeatedly ignoring their requirements.

You may believe you are talking to the customer when you speak to the "corporate" representative who "buys" the "corporate requirements" for an organization. But the customer is also those hundreds of other users who need the opportunity to talk to you. (Incidentally, this means actually talk, not "fill in a form.")

American Express can take some consolation in the fact that among financial institutions they do better than most of the British banking industry when it comes to listening to the customer. The arrogance of British banks is legendary, and their fees are exorbitant. In this light, I was delighted to see Martin Taylor, my former chairman at Courtaulds, appointed chief executive of Barclays. He is a leader who understands the importance of listening to the customer and delivering customer value. I switched my U.K. business to Barclays after dealing with another bank, which switched off its fax machine at 5:00 p.m. U.K. time. Clearly, they did not wish to be part of the global marketplace! In all industries the global marketplace makes it possible for the customer to go elsewhere.

CUSTOMERS MUST TELL THEIR SUPPLIERS . . .

When you, as a customer, receive poor service in a restaurant, at a bank, or on a (so-called) customer service line, the organization you are dealing with is showing disrespect for your business. They are treating you as if you're getting in the way of their day going smoothly. If they *don't* want your business, do them and yourself a favor and take your business elsewhere. It is your responsibility as a customer to *insist* on proper service. If you do not take action, you let the problem get worse, which does no one any good. Yes, I get angry when I get treated poorly as a customer. You should too.

As your business grows, it is critical that you keep in touch with the people who speak to your customers, and it is critical that the business leader hears both the good news and the bad news of customer feedback. You must hear what the sales people are saying, but must continue to listen to the customer directly. Whether you have small clients or large, you must also hear the messages which come from the client's receiving dock and accounts payable office, as well as all the other moments of truth.

You can see that your customers' expectations, or their requirements, involve every aspect of your business. What is done by each member of your organization affects the customers' opinion of your organization, and it affects whether they wish to continue giving you their business.

If an organization has dissatisfied customers, less than 5 percent of these customers complain. Instead, the unhappy customers usually go away, and well over 50 percent of them will tell someone else about their bad experience. Customers are expecting better products and services every day, and now demand assurance that your organization can meet their requirements.

You must hear the messages that come from the people who fly on your airline, rent your automobile, or wear the uniform that you supply.

A UNIFORM EXCEPTION, A SHINING EXAMPLE

Cadet Uniform Services may be a company you have never heard of. As finalists in the Canadian Awards for Business Excellence, they rubbed shoulders with major international corporations such as Allied Signal. In fact, this small Canadian company has an enviable customer *retention* rate of 99.4 percent in an industry that rarely reaches 80 percent.

Cadet's secret is not remarkable. They talk to the customer, and listen to the replies. They constantly measure their customer service. They recognize that the most frequent customer interface is not through the salesperson who gets the order, but through the delivery driver who delivers the customer service every day of the week. Cadet's competitors employ drivers; Cadet employs Customer Service Representatives (CSRs). The CSR constantly extracts information on customer needs, and is rewarded accordingly. The CSR also delivers what the customer needs. During the great blizzard of January 1993, which brought Toronto to a standstill, every one of these remarkable people delivered to their customers, because they believed in the customers, and in Cadet's commitment to the customers. Arnold Gedmintas, who runs the operation at Cadet, listens avidly to the messages that come from the customer. This is the priceless information Cadet uses to generate even greater customer satisfaction.

Windsor, Ontario, is known as the Canadian Rose City, because of the friendly climate. The business climate is not so cordial. Windsor sits across the river from Detroit, Michigan, the Motor City. As the North American Free Trade Agreement (NAFTA) has approached, suppliers to the motor industry see an increasing threat. Valiant Machine and Tool Inc. makes high-tech robotics and machine tools for the motor industry, and has grown dramatically in the face of NAFTA, and during the recession of the early 1990s. In 1992, Valiant was awarded "Company of the Year" in Windsor. The leader of this dramatic growth is Michael Solcz, Sr., who is a gentleman in every sense of the word. Michael talks constantly to his customers, and listens to what the customer says. He listens to what his salespeople say, and he uses this knowledge to drive the strategic plan of the organization.

All of this knowledge that you gain from the customer should feed into your strategic quality plan, and drive both your process improvement and your people improvement. Blanton Godfrey of the Juran Institute, speaking at the Toronto ASQC Forum in 1993, revealed that research had shown that less than 20 percent of organizations use their shortcomings in customer product or service to drive improvement. Most hope and wish that problems will either go away, or at least not come back again.

Identify all of your customer interfaces (moments of truth) and ask yourself when you last asked the people in your organization what difficulties they experience in meeting their customer requirements. Ask yourself what opportunity those people have to input their difficulties to the strategic quality plan. Ask yourself whether that input gets dismissed, devalued, or destroyed before it arrives at the plan.

Finally, a word of warning. Small organizations are especially vulnerable to waste and chaos caused by leaders who pride themselves on being customer responsive. I have seen so many companies that have grown successfully to employing, say, 40 to 50 people, and are driven by the great entrepreneurial spirit of their leader. At this point, the leader is starting to lose contact with what is happening in the guts of the business, and retains the image of when it was 10 or 15 employees. Sudden changes in requirements by the external customer or client no longer are handled in the same way. Failure to get client requirements agreed on up front has a destructive effect on internal morale, and is a major cause of the onset of waste and rework. This issue will be revisited in the chapters on process ownership and cost of quality.

As I've talked about companies like Cadet Uniform Services and Valiant, you have hopefully started to form a picture in your mind of what you would like your new company to look like. Remember again C.S. Wallace, Jr., who talked about the benchmarking his company had done, and said, "You can call it benchmarking; I call it 'kinda copyin.'" Looking at the good practices of other companies is one of the first foundation steps as you start to create the vision of the company you want to be.

BROWSER'S BRIEFING

- All business leaders must know who their customer(s) are, and must talk to them continuously.
- Leaders include the president, the manufacturing manager, the financial controller—and anyone who may be "frightened" of the customer.
- When customer contact is delegated, communications with the "delegatee" must be treated like a fragile fiber optic.
- We must also talk to our customer's customer to eliminate the risk of distorted communication.
- Our suppliers are as important as our customers.
- If your customers have bad experiences, over 50 percent will tell another of your potential customers, and less than 5 percent will tell you.
- Despite its rare value, only 20 percent of companies use customer feedback information to drive business improvement.
- All of your customer interfaces must be identified, and the delivery performance (product and service) must be measured.
- Customers will not and should not "fill out forms" for your convenience. You need to actually listen to them.
- Large organizations suffer from the leadership being distanced from the customer.
- Smaller organizations suffer from the leadership thinking that "customer responsiveness" means throwing their organizations into chaos, when in fact the customer loses from this behavior in the long term.
- Look for companies who deal with their customers well (perhaps your own suppliers?). Copy their best practices.

PART II

THE FOUNDATION

3 | The Vision

"Begin with the end in mind."
—Stephen Covey

"The future is very important ... it is where we will spend the rest of our lives."
—Joel Arthur Barker

So, you are embarking on a journey to become a better organization. Do you know where you are heading? Do you have a vision, a picture of the future?

In 1979, my family and I bought a 100-year-old cottage in an old English village named Prestbury. The roof leaked, the windows were rotten, the kitchen had an old crock sink, and the bath was so old, it actually turned out to have some antique value. We bought the house because the village was one of the prettiest in England, and the house was of the beautiful Cheshire half-timbered style. It was appropriately named Hope Cottage.

Over the next three to four years, we labored, retiling the roof, installing the new windows which replicated the originals, and refitting the kitchen and bathroom with units that were in keeping with a late Victorian country house.

The ideas for restoration came from countless sources. Copies of *House and Garden, Casa Vogue,* and *Interiors* gave the ethereal mood of the future residence. Copies of home improvement magazines gave the practical how-to information. Visits to houses of friends doing similar restorations gave hope when ours faded. Television programs, visits to furnishing stores, decorations in old country pubs: all of these sources helped build the picture of our "Dream Home."

This picture of the house as it would be in the future was our vision. This is what maintained the "pull forward" when times got tough.

SHARING THE VISION

I wish I could go on to say that I shared this vision and agreed on it with my family. I had my own clear picture of the Hope Cottage of the future, my wife had hers, and my daughters had a different one again. Rachel and Sarah knew the colors and pictures they wanted in their bedrooms, and the swing and seesaw they wanted in the garden. My wife had her wish list for the kitchen and the living room. My priority was the new roof, the garage, and the living room extension at the back of the house.

Hindsight is 20/20, and one of the lessons I have learned in later years is the importance of sharing and agreeing on the vision the organization is working towards.

Taking time to share our pictures of the future would have spared us much of the stress and tension in the first three to four years of restoration. If every member of the family had seen their picture fit into the plan—if every member of the family had even had a clear picture, or vision, at all—then they would have been able to contribute to the restoration process with much more energy and enthusiasm.

Instead, I worked enormous hours, called on old favors from friends, and relied on the fact that my family would trust me because of my enormous commitment to the work at hand. Whenever a leader says "Trust me," then it is a sure sign of failed communication. You don't ask for trust; it is only given for free.

RENOVATING YOUR ORGANIZATION

If all this sounds a little bit familiar, then you have recognized that you are about to engage in a building or restoration process in your own organization, and that having a clear and shared vision of the future is critical for everyone in the organization.

Any process that involves change will test people's trust in you. You are asking them to enter the unknown. The more you can remove the mystery and build a positive image of the future, the more secure they will feel with the journey you are undertaking.

However, you're not dealing with a family of four. There will be many more different perspectives of that picture of the future.

One of the best organizations I know at creating and communicating its vision of the future is Cadet Uniform Services, mentioned in Chapter 2. Anyone who walks into Cadet can feel service quality coming out of the walls. The president, Quentin Wahl, is both a remarkable visionary and a practical person. His right-hand man, Arnold Gedmintas, is both a people person and a detailed number cruncher. These two men have detailed and executed their vision of an organization that does it right the first time by constantly exploring the world for role models, and constantly talking with their own people and sharing their own vision and enthusiasm for the future.

THE "RETREAT" APPROACH TO VISIONING

A lot of management teams believe a weekend in the lake country among the birds and the trees, reflecting on beautiful thoughts, is what visioning is all about. This frees the minds of task-oriented business leaders who need to take some time to stand back and look at their own organizations.

The retreat is an important way of initiating a visioning process. I once conducted one of these visioning sessions in the beautiful lake country of the Muskokas in southeast Ontario. A retreat is a "loose-tight" kind of activity. It's loose in the sense that you must remove the shackles of daily business, and the right environment releases the mind and fosters team bonding. However, there must be a structure and direction to maintain the left-brain influence.

The organization I was working with on this occasion was a government aviation department facing privatization. We started the two days with a lot of fear, and finished with a lot of excitement as the future opportunities were recognized.

Visioning in Stages

The first stages in visioning are to get a clear sense of where you are now. What are your key processes, who are your customers, and what do you deliver to them? You then move on to look at what's important to your own organization, and what's important to your customers. What are your own values, and what are your customer's requirements? This gets you into a position to be thinking of what the differences are between the way you do things now, and the way you will do them in the new organization.

This government department saw the main differences as speed, the type of employees they had, being more competitive, and having less bureaucracy. They were then in a position to start building their vision of a more aggressive and competitive organization, which was more forward thinking, cost effective, and customer focused. I remember Bob Middleton, one of the team members, sitting back at the end of the session and saying, "This is going to be a pretty impressive organization to work for!"

Visioning is a continuous activity, and it needs to be led by the senior people. In many organizations, leaders neither communicate their vision to the rest of the people in the organization, nor do they listen to their hopes and aspirations. In Chapter 8, you will find a discussion about depth and span of communication. Your own visioning will not penetrate more than three layers down in your organization, and you must work constantly, listening to what people out there want the organization to be, as well as communicating your own inspiration of the future to the people around you.

We will keep coming back to the importance of good communication, and we'll talk in detail about the concepts of communication in

Chapter 15. For the moment, though, let's look at some of the practical things we should do to communicate a vision of the future.

DEVELOPING THE VISION

If you're not satisfied with where you are now, then you need to decide where you would like to be. If you ask everyone in your organization what they would like the organization to become, you may hear back a positive, more detailed version of the descriptions on pages 15 and 16 of Chapter 1:

• Survival	*becomes*	a healthier organization
• The customer	*becomes*	less complaints
• Increased market share	*becomes*	more business
• More profit	*becomes*	more salary and benefits

These initial responses are the gut reactions of people venting pent-up frustration. This is bound to happen when people get asked for the first time, "What would you like your organization to look/feel/be like?" Too many businesses do this through an impersonal survey published by the human resource department, and are disappointed at the response.

One of the best times to assess people's thoughts and feelings is during your quality education. This is also the time to show people some role models of organizations you would like to emulate.

Why should the senior managers be the only ones to visit companies who have succeeded in quality? Over a 12-month period, you should have everyone visit at least one organization that is succeeding in quality. These companies are not hard to find, and one of the remarkable things about people who succeed in quality is that they want to tell the world about it. The American Society for Quality Control (ASQC) is a good source of information here, and your own industry links with customers, suppliers, and competitors will be another source. Share your own "good practices" with these companies, and you will gradually build a network of companies with whom you can "benchmark." Choose your companies for specific reasons, and have teams from your own company go with a plan and return to a thorough debriefing. My friends at Cadet Uniform share constantly with a company in Cincinnati in the same line of business, just as I visited friends and old houses while rebuilding Hope Cottage.

SUCCESS BREEDS SUCCESS

You also need to read the equivalent of *Home and Garden* or *Casa Vogue,* as I did in Hope Cottage. Give people books to read. Not weighty tomes; people like quick reads. But reading books is only one part of the visioning process. Remember, different people like different styles of writing, and some people don't like reading at all. I recall in the 1980s some company presidents who were inspired by Philip Crosby's *Quality Is Free* bought copies for everyone in their organizations. They wondered why nothing changed, even though Crosby's style appeals to many.

Audio cassette tapes are one of your most powerful communication media. They're a wonderful way of building your vision of a quality organization, and many books these days are in cassette form. Use videos too. Show people videos of successful quality organizations at least once a month. Discuss what they see and like, and what they don't like.

All these activities help people to learn what a successful organization looks like, and start to build goals in their minds for both themselves and the organization. In *The Fifth Discipline,* Peter Senge quotes Arie de Geus, head of planning for Royal Dutch/Shell, who said, "The ability to learn faster than your competitors may be the only sustainable advantage (Senge 1990, 4)."

If you play golf, tennis, or any other sport, you know that one of the best ways to improve is to mix with better players. Choose your business playing partners carefully, and have everyone in your organization do some "imagineering," in which they visualize what their own job, their own department, and their own organization will look like when you become a quality organization.

Yes, do the executive retreats as well, but remember to move beyond that and involve everyone. This way, you are building the picture for everyone, and visualizing the culture you want in your organization.

BROWSER'S BRIEFING

- *"The future is very important ... it is where we will spend the rest of our lives."*—Joel Arthur Barker
- As with our personal lives, our organization must have a clear sense of direction, or we will be the victim of fate, rather than the beneficiary of good fortune.
- Build your picture of your future organization by looking at other successes.
- Build on other people's successes by "imagineering."
- Build and share the vision with everybody in the organization. Be prepared to spend "real time" doing this.
- The words "trust me" indicate you have failed to communicate in the visioning process.
- Most leaders can communicate successfully to a range of six to eight people, and to a depth of three layers in their organizations.
- Collect everyone's thoughts and feelings on what they want your organization to look like, to feel like, to be like.
- One of the best times to do this collecting is during the initial quality education.
- Have *everyone* visit their corresponding department/function in another successful organization at least once in a year.
- Read books. Listen to audio tapes. Watch videos. Meet people who are successful.
- *"The ability to learn faster than your competitors may be the only sustainable advantage."*—Arie de Geus
- Evaluate your capacity to change and strengthen your weaknesses.

4 Culture

We're all different...

Perhaps the best example of a quality culture that I have encountered is at Cadet Uniform Services. In the summer of 1992, the local section of the American Society for Quality Control (ASQC), a society of quality professionals, visited Cadet as part of its regular meeting program. Without exception, these people came away from Cadet overwhelmed. People said, "You could actually feel quality coming out of the walls." At Cadet, you immediately sense the trust between people, and yet you feel the drive for ever-improving customer service. Any new employee joining Cadet is thoroughly interviewed by at least four and sometimes up to ten different people. If the potential employee "measures up," they are asked to study the values which Cadet sees as fundamental, and if they agree, then they are asked to sign that agreement. Cadet didn't get to this position overnight, though. Like other companies that have developed a quality organization, there were failures on the way. All organizations that have developed a quality organization did it by changing, and by using a change process.

I spent many years in the Courtaulds Group, which was so large that the "culture" varied across the different parts of the group. In some parts of the group, people believed in helping each other, in sharing knowledge, and in the greater good of the successful team. I have lifelong friends from the department of chemical engineering, where I first worked. The department was created by Frank (later Sir Frank and finally Lord) Kearton. Frank Kearton was feared and yet respected; he was tough, but he was forthright. He created a line of succession based on skill and ability. Recruitment into the department was carried out with deep scrutiny of all applicants. I remember meeting the great man at a later stage in my career and still carry the memory of his ability to see right into people. He chose the right people for the culture he wanted, and the culture survived generations of department heads.

In my later years in the group, I worked in an area where people were preoccupied with personal survival. They were always trying to catch the chairman's ear, and information or knowledge was jealously guarded as a source of power.

CULTURE AND SHARED VALUES

In 1987, after 22 years, I left Courtaulds, and was privileged to work in an organization created by Phil Crosby. I felt privileged because the people I worked with wanted to help me and while they all possessed an awesome level of skill and knowledge, they had no need to prove it to the people they worked with.

Phil Crosby personally interviewed everyone who joined the organization, and identified whether they had the right set of values. Every interviewee met up to ten different Crosby people before joining and the organization cross-referenced all interviewees.

Again, I have formed long-lasting friendships with people I knew at Crosby. We shared the same principles and values, and still do.

Do you see the commonality with the Courtaulds department of chemical engineering? To develop the culture you want, you must have total buy-in to your values from your senior managers, and you must ensure total commitment to those values with any new person joining the organization, and ultimately everyone else in the organization.

I had left Courtaulds after spending several years in another part of the business, where the culture was very different. I left because my *basic values* were being compromised continuously, and I was changing into a person I no longer respected. I was becoming a chameleon, capable of shifting to fit any situation. I didn't realize this at the time, only in hindsight. The turnover of senior managers in this part of the business had become very high.

The internal failure of that part of Courtaulds was masked by external commercial success. Household textiles were a boom segment of the British economy during the 1980s. Even though customer service was appalling, the customer was so hungry for the product that no serious effort was made to eliminate the root cause of bad service. A glance at the competition showed what could have been achieved, and the competition wasn't too spectacular either!

In the chapter on vision you probably started to build a picture of the company you'd like to be. There are many things you do already which are good, and many things others do which are better. We are starting to talk about change, and a fundamental change in the way we do business. This means a change in our company behavior, and our behavior is based on those values or principles we believe are important. Our company culture is the values, beliefs, and behaviors which our company has learned over time.

However, in the same way as a company has a culture, so does each member of the company come from a family that has its own culture, and those same people reflect the culture of the nation in which they company operates. Bringing together both the national culture and the family culture of the company members provides the business with a real challenge as it starts to change its culture to one in which a belief in quality is a prime value.

A common factor in the organizations I have described is the strength of the leaders. You may be saying you're not Phil Crosby or Frank Kearton. Most of us aren't, but the distinctive feature of these people was a clear set of values which they adhered to, day in and day out, as did the people immediately surrounding them. You don't have to be a big name to be a good leader.

During part of the time I was in the household textile division of Courtaulds, I ran the sales operation of Christy Towels. In the U.K., the Christy brand has an 80 percent recognition factor in the male population, and nearly 100 percent in the female population. The humble towel had been invented by William Miller Christy after visiting the harem of the Sultan of Turkey and seeing a strange loop pile fabric being woven by hand. Queen Victoria purchased the first six dozen towels at the Great Exhibition of 1851 and Christy has produced "quality" Royal Turkish Towels ever since. With this kind of reputation, you'd think the job of sales manager was a sinecure.

Not so. The brand had become debased in the 1970s through wide price variations and poor designs, and while the consumer still thought of Christy as "the best," the retailer had built a deep mistrust and no longer stocked the product. A man with strong personal values was given the job of reviving the dying animal.

Gordon Johnson is someone you've probably never heard of. As general manager, he created a culture at Christy based on pride and trust. As sales manager, I communicated the integrity inside the organization to the external customer in terms of price integrity, and we put design back into the product by listening to what the customer wanted. More importantly, the external customer sensed the internal culture of the organization, and trusted us with their business. Christy Towels became an oasis of trust and respect inside the larger business division, where the values included neither respect for the individual nor respect for the customer.

Gordon withstood the barrage of dishonest practices around him, and people inside Christy respected him for this.

THE DESIRE TO CHANGE CULTURE

Perhaps the culture that is most often discussed, and least understood, is the IBM culture. I remember, many years back, someone saying to me about IBM people, "They eat their dead." I carried this image of nine-foot-tall blue-suited cannibals for many years. Later, as I got to know IBM people, I found a few who did actually "bleed blue," and were committed to their company, but they were committed because their company was committed to them. Thomas Watson's "respect for the individual" credo was deeply rooted in the organization. I cannot begin to describe one of the strongest company cultures of our time in this short space, but when faced with the decision in 1992 to change or die,

IBM chose to change. Taking on Lou Gerstner as CEO showed a clear commitment to change many of its outdated practices, in a world where more flexibility is needed.

CULTURE CLASH

A word of warning: it is very easy to crush a culture that is based on trust and respect, and is customer-focused. Christy Towels was absorbed into a larger organization, and within four years a mill that had successfully served the customer for 140 years was dead. The name survives, but does the soul? The good news is that Gordon Johnson kept his values, if not his job. The bad news is that 200 people in Manchester joined the lengthening British unemployment queue.

Across the world from Manchester, the Crosby organization in the United States was purchased in 1989. The British press quoted the purchaser, Lord Stevens of Ludgate, as saying that a "softer image" was wanted for his own organization. He regarded Crosby as having the type of company culture which people aspire to. Reading a contract of employment for these new owners will tell you about its company culture. They were very concerned about their reputation in many parts of the marketplace. Four years later, about 30 of the 300 people in Crosby at the time of the takeover remained. The senior management of the new owners had no desire to change their culture. They had succeeded in the old culture, and were certainly not going to jeopardize their success.

The biggest cause of failure in company mergers or takeovers is the clash of cultures.

WHAT CULTURE DO YOU WANT?

If you are developing a vision of a successful organization in which people "do it right the first time," then you have to decide what kind of people you expect to see in your organization. You need to decide how you will behave. You will see that people's skills or "core competencies" are a key part of that vision. As we get deeper into looking into what happens in successful quality organizations we will see that mutual trust and respect, customer focus, and a desire to do things better are the kind of things that drive people's behavior. These are examples of "quality values," and that leads us to define, in the next chapter, the values on which a quality culture is based.

BROWSER'S BRIEFING

- Your vision will show your company doing things in certain ways. Some of these practices will be different from present ones.
- The way you do things is a reflection of your culture. If you are going to change the way you do things, you are going to change your culture.
- Cultures vary between families, between companies, and between nations. Your company culture will reflect your national culture, and the culture of the families that your people come from.
- "Benchmarking" successful organizations will show the behaviors that encourage success.
- Behaviors such as secrecy, politicking, pursuit of self-interest, and interdepartmental sabotage will make single departments successful.
- These behaviors will also make other departments fail.
- For the organization to succeed, all departments must succeed.
- Organizational failure is often masked by commercial "windows of opportunity," which produce a short-term profit.
- Recruit new people who will behave in accordance with the behavior patterns you want to encourage.
- The leadership of your organization are the role models for the culture you aspire to. The leadership must buy into and practice the culture you wish to create.
- The evidence shows that for long-term success, a culture must encourage behaviors such as trust and respect between people, increasing and sharing knowledge, continuously improving performance, and satisfying the ultimate customer.
- A culture must have a desire to continuously change and improve.

5 Quality Values

The founding fathers of the United States wrote, "We hold these truths to be self-evident; that all men are created equal..." This was a clear break with the European class system. English expatriates who revisit their homeland see how the class system is fundamentally woven into all daily transactions, and yet many English hold on to and value that system.

Canadians have created a culture which is unique in the world, and yet few Canadians are able to define their culture or values. At the first breath of spring, the Canadian wants to go north and be among the birds, the trees, the animals, and the lakes. The Canadian has a deep love for animals, and this was acquired from the native people. Many Americans, on the other hand, want to go hunting.

My wife is of Italian descent; my family is English. The English have a basic belief that one should *Never hit a man when he is down;* the Italian view is that *If you want to win, then the best time to attack is when your opponent is down.* This is only one value difference between the two nations. Take a moment to think about the stresses that arose as we tried to integrate our two cultures in the early months of marriage.

AGREEING ON BASIC VALUES

Different values are neither right or wrong, but they are different. The problem arises when one person says he or she is right and the other disagrees. If people are going to work in harmony, some common values need to be agreed upon.

If you are embarking on a quality journey, you must agree upon some basic quality values. Don't make the list too long, and don't make value statements too complicated. This is not a philosophical ego trip for the "thinkers" on the management team. These are basic principles which you will ask everyone in your company to buy into.

Unless you take time to agree on these basic beliefs and values, then I can promise you endless internal conflict. You only have to look at why nations go to war to see that differences in values are the root cause of much of humanity's disagreement.

If you have evaluated where you are now and have built a vision of where you would like to be, you are probably left with a large gap between those two points. Your cost of quality assessment may have found that the annual budgeting process is a major time waster, an ISO 9000 audit may have shown the need for a corrective action system, and your employee survey may have revealed a weak communications system. This is the gap that you need to traverse on your quality journey.

At this point many people jump into what is called "gap analysis." But before getting too deeply into gap analysis, it is important to stop and ask the very basic questions, like:

- *What are our basic beliefs?*

- *What are our quality values?*

Some would argue that this should be done sooner, but I believe that first engaging in the self-assessment and visioning activities will flush out your beliefs and values, allowing a consensus to be reached much more easily at this stage. Consensus on your values is vital if the ensuing quality process is to be a success. Phil Crosby did an excellent job in this regard with his Four Absolutes of Quality. Company leaders who started their quality journey back in the 1980s and used his Four Absolutes gave everyone in their organization some basic values to believe in. Thomas Watson, Sr., back in the early days of IBM, gave the organization its Basic Beliefs of respect for the individual, best possible service to the customer, and performing every task in a superior manner.

VALUES: THE FOUNDATION OF A CULTURE

Values and beliefs are the foundation of our culture, and in the same way that a nation has a culture, so does a company. This is often hard to understand in a small company which has grown from a single entrepreneurial idea. In the early days when survival was the number one issue, all you did was go out there and get the business. Often, medium and larger companies have not stopped to think about the basic values that are the foundation of their culture, especially if their growth has been rapid and successful.

Take a moment to think of some of the value differences between nations. The values are rarely written down, but they fundamentally influence the thinking of the peoples.

People like Philip Crosby, Thomas Watson, Sr., Joseph Juran, and W. Edwards Deming give us some good thinking here. As a starting point, let's look at a basic definition of quality.

WHO DEFINES QUALITY: A BASIC VALUE

We've already talked about quality being defined by the customer, and yet many people do not have this basic value. Instead, they believe quality has to be defined by the supplier of the product or service. Crosby's definition of quality is "conformance to requirements." Juran talks about "fitness for purpose." There are many other definitions, but they all boil down to delivering to the customer what the customer wants. The definition I happen to prefer is *"conformance to agreed upon customer requirements."*

You will find people in your organization who have different definitions of quality, and some will hold a deep-seated belief that quality is synonymous with high expense. When I give seminars, I show the participants an expensive gold-plated pen that was bought for me by my daughter for over $100. I treasure this pen, and few would disagree that it is a "quality" pen. I then show them a felt tip marker, which I use on the flip chart, and which costs about one dollar. For writing on a flip chart, the felt tip pen is the "quality" pen—writing from the expensive pen my daughter gave me would be barely visible. It would not conform to my customers' requirements. I find these days that few people who have been exposed to quality have a problem with this definition, but if you are going to adopt this basic value into your new company culture, you will have to educate all your employees to the definition of quality as conformance to customer requirements.

RESPECT FOR THE INDIVIDUAL

When Thomas Watson, Sr., included "respect for the individual" among the Basic Beliefs of IBM, he acknowledged that many businesses are driven by fear, applied through "abuse of the individual." People give their best when they are enthusiastic, and they add greater value when they use their minds as well as their bodies. Whatever the mood inside your organization, you will not be able to hide it from your customer. You need to ask yourself if your vision of the organization includes happy people or people driven by fear.

If you have a group of people who are positive, respectful of each other, and striving to meet the customer's requirements, then the basic value of continuous improvement will come so much more easily. The tough part about continuous improvement is that when you've worked hard to build prevention through procedures, you feel reluctant to change anything. The leadership in the organization can demonstrate its true commitment to quality by a daily involvement in the improvement of the most needful business processes. Probably the best remembered of Deming's 14 Points is "Drive out fear."

THE VALUE OF EDUCATION

We are now starting to take on an obligation to find the customer's requirements and to agree with our customer on our ability to meet those requirements. We are also starting to see another value emerging: the need to continuously train and educate people in an organization. In Chapter 3, I quoted Arie de Geus of Royal Dutch/Shell, who suggested that the only sustainable competitive edge an organization has is its ability to learn more rapidly than the competition.

THE VALUE OF PREVENTION

Now a much deeper value starts to emerge, and it is perhaps the most all-encompassing value in quality. Developing a mind-set of prevention throughout the organization will probably do more to enable you to meet your customer's requirements than any other change you make in your culture. Philip Crosby talks about prevention as the system to deliver quality. If you look at the 1994 revision of the ISO 9000 standards, you will notice a fundamental shift in key words away from appraisal or correction and toward prevention. If you follow the Baldrige criteria, you must move away from a reactive response to the customer and toward a prevention-oriented culture.

This is probably the most emotional shift the entrepreneurial business leader has to deal with. If this describes you, then you have probably built a highly successful organization based on your ability to *respond to the customer*. So far, so good; but that word *respond* is no longer good enough. You are probably one of the fastest tap dancers in the business, and you have recruited a team who can follow your steps and even predict your next move. Guessing will not work any more. Intuition is a key part of your success, past, present, and future, but intuition is not magic; it is a highly developed skill we will talk about in Chapter 15, on communication.

Prevention is what your customers have asked for in the past, and will *demand* in the future. It means having business processes that are capable of *doing it right the first time,* and people who no longer have an attitude that *we can put it right later.* Prevention means thinking ahead—no longer responding to the customer but rather being proactive and delighting the customer. Prevention means that you have to work with your team, and each player has to *know* his or her part in delivering to the customer.

The biggest enemy of prevention is time. I have a bookmark from a little gift shop in Vermont which says, "Never enough time to do it right;

always enough time to do it over." Grandma used to say it, and it still holds true today.

How Do We Make Prevention Happen?

Taking time up front to agree on requirements with our customer is one of the first preventive behaviors. We'll see later that establishing clear process ownership in your organization will be a prerequisite for prevention. Secondly, taking time to talk to your suppliers and ensure they understand your requirements is the next step in building prevention. We'll also explore this further in Chapter 10, on process ownership. This is where the Japanese have been so effective over the last several decades. Get into the niggling details here and you save much heartache later. The problem is that usually customers do not know their requirements, and as they learn more about your capabilities, they ask for things they did not think about at the outset.

The company sales staff has a critical role here, and yet I see so many organizations where the sales force is not included in the quality process, and the sales people do not understand the huge cost to the organization (and hence the customer) when they overlook a requirement.

The Equipment Myth

Applying prevention to our business processes is where the big strides are made.

Many people say that if they only had better equipment that did it right the first time, there would be far fewer problems; yet the general experience is that equipment is the most blamed and the least guilty.

Roger Milliken, whose company won the Baldrige Award, started his quality journey in 1980. The Japanese were destroying him in the marketplace, and yet he had state-of-the-art machinery. He visited Japan and discovered top companies using equipment as much as 20 years old. The secret? Training and following procedures. We'll talk about training in Chapter 14, and discuss procedures in Chapter 21. Moving beyond prevention takes us to the next value of continuous improvement.

CONTINUOUS IMPROVEMENT

Masaaki Imai, the author of *Kaizen*, has a saying: *"Everyone has two jobs. The first is doing their job, and the second is improving the way they do their job."* Everyone in the organization has to be looking for a better way, but traditionally, this has often been done in isolation by a few individuals. A quality organization has people working together, and not making unilateral changes that will affect others in a negative fashion. The goal is for people to accept a change generated elsewhere because they recognize it to be to the greater benefit of everyone. The desire to continuously improve is a fundamental value in all quality organizations.

A POLICY OR VALUE STATEMENT

Having drawn up your value statement, it is important to present it in a statement of commitment. This is usually called a *quality policy*.

Make these values simple and easy to understand. Don't wrap them up in fancy words or conceptual jargon. Wrap them together in your policy statement on quality. Your policy statement should be short and to the point, and with no compromises. The Ten Commandments received by Moses can be stated in fewer than 100 English words.

I've seen quality policy statements running to 300 and 500 words and looking as though they were designed by a committee of lawyers. Who in the organization is even interested in a statement like that? No wonder people in the company do not understand where their company is going.

SO WHERE DO WE GO NOW?

So did you take that time to build your vision and values, and do you have a clear and concise policy statement, and have you built the vision in the minds of everyone in the organization?

Maybe you did, but you're not sure whether everyone in the organization understands. Have you asked? Have you checked? Do they know whether you are going to Berlin, Paris, or Rome?

If you are clear where you want to be, do you know how you're going to get there? Most organizations think that if they educate everyone (teach them how to drive) and give them a tool box (SPC, fishbone diagrams, process model), people will drive confidently and excitedly down the highway, arriving simultaneously at the chosen city. It doesn't happen that way, does it?

You do need a vehicle to get you to your chosen destination of being a quality organization. The half-dozen people who lead your organization need to learn how to drive this vehicle first, and they should become good enough drivers to teach their own immediate staff.

This vehicle is going to be called the "change process." It's the process you will operate to change your organization from an uncoordinated, crisis-riddled, money waster, to that vision of an organization whose people do things right the first time (not the second time) and where you are able to respond to your customers and keep them happy all the time.

Did you have a change process when you started your quality journey? Perhaps you did, but there were so many obstacles on your highway that you never really got started. What are the obstacles to making change happen in your organization? We'll look at these in Chapter 6.

B R O W S E R ' S   B R I E F I N G

- Before moving to the "new culture," it is important to assess where you are now.
- The values, or basic beliefs, of an organization will define the way people do things, or their behaviors.
- Philip Crosby gave organizations his Four Absolutes. Thomas Watson, Sr., gave IBM that company's Basic Beliefs.
- Lack of agreement on values leads to conflict, and to people in the organization pulling in different directions.
- As businesses and organizations become global, it becomes essential to take account of the cultural variations among nations as they affect different parts of the global organization.
- An organization committed to quality has to be clear that the customer is the final arbiter of quality.
- Investment in people and development of their skills is a value held by all long-term successful organizations.
- The ultimate value in quality is prevention. The application of prevention to all business processes is the only way the customer can be assured of receiving what you have promised.
- Prevention must, however, be a dynamic activity, and continuous improvement has to be applied to all business activities.
- Successful organizations are not satisfied with the status quo, and seek to continuously improve.
- To make these values part of an organization's way of life, a change in culture is required, and the culture change requires a change process.

PART III

THE CHANGE

6 | Resistance to Change

Change can be exhilarating, or change can be scary. Visualize owning a red Porsche and driving it on a German *autobahn* (a four-lane highway) at 120 mph. If you like speed (and for "speed" you can read "change"), then the experience is exhilarating. Close your eyes and imagine how it feels. Now imagine yourself in the passenger seat. In the driver's seat is someone you know but don't entirely trust, or who has lost interest in the experience! You're still doing 120 mph. Close your eyes again and capture your feelings now! The majority of people in the organization feel like you felt in that passenger seat: terrified! They are not in control of their destiny, and no one will even tell them what will happen next.

LEARNING HOW TO DRIVE

You have to start the change process slowly. Leaders of the business have to learn how to drive the vehicle before it gathers speed. Then they have to learn to share the driving with others in their organization if they want everyone to participate in the change process.

Many senior managers I have encountered think they know how to drive. They haven't taken the time to learn to do it well and they certainly don't recognize that change is a new and different vehicle. This journey is going to match you against world class drivers. It's not a Sunday drive in the country. The management team must all learn how to be world class drivers eventually, but they will be taking the vehicle on the road immediately.

Next, most managers have a different picture of where they are going. Some think the *autobahn* goes to Berlin, others believe the *autoroute* heads for Paris, and yet others think the *autostrada* is bound for Rome. People don't even know what the destination looks like. Are the buildings 20 years old in Berlin, 200 years old in Paris, or 2,000 years old in Rome? Is the weather blue skies or snow? Is the temperature freezing, or hot and humid?

On the other hand, many chief executives believe they already have a wonderful culture and don't see the need for change. You must face the reality that your own company culture can always become better suited to encouraging quality to happen. Otherwise, you wouldn't have a problem delivering quality. In reality, it probably could be a *lot* better suited to making quality happen.

Do you trust and respect the people who work with you? Do you recruit people who are compatible with the culture you are moving toward?

Look again at the reasons why you are not able to deliver quality at the moment. In the opening chapter, we saw that the main reasons were:

1. Poor communication

2. Unclear and changing requirements

3. Lack of senior management commitment

4. Employee cynicism and poor morale

5. Lack of training

6. Bad suppliers

7. Not sticking to procedures

8. Quick fixes

9. Lack of time

10. Lack of process ownership

You'd think that with a list like this, changing things would be easy—yet over 70 percent of the organizations that have tried TQM have not had the results they wanted.

You and the people in your organization have the in-depth knowledge to identify your own reasons for failure.

However, the number one reason for failure, time and again, is resistance to change, which can be rewritten to read "fear of change."

RESISTANCE AT EVERY LEVEL

Fear of change comes at all levels in the organization, and at different times in the quality improvement process.

The company president fears that the company, "his baby," will change into some Frankensteinian monster he doesn't recognize. His resistance is subtle, and is achieved through that wonderfully legitimate tool called delegation.

The vice presidents are the real crisis managers, and their career success has come through dealing with the abundance of crises the company has generated over the years. Subconsciously, they may drag their heels on removing the root causes of the company's problems.

The middle managers and supervisors are the *most* threatened by change. Their traditional role has been that of the dictatorial coach, telling people what to do and when. They are soon going to be asked to go out on the field and participate. "Can I still even catch or kick the ball?" they ask. Resistance here is often the most damaging and these are often the most skilled and experienced people you have. Those skills and that experience need to be focused into the new change process. More attention needs to be paid to this group of people than almost any other. They need to develop new skills, new knowledge.

The clerical and operational staff will embrace change with the greatest welcome, but will be the most skeptical about whether management is truly committed.

Nearly everyone I've talked to or whose material I've read agrees that resistance to change is the biggest obstacle to making quality happen. You may be saying, "But I thought lack of top management commitment was the biggest obstacle." For "lack of commitment," read "passive resistance or loss of interest in change."

This is why you must create a clear and simple picture or vision of where you are going. If you want to be a quality organization, then what does a quality organization look like? Don't give people conceptual or abstract pictures like, "We will all be prevention-oriented and conform to customer requirements while striving for continuous improvement." This is a "consensus" statement from a management team who argue all morning about their vision.

Remember the advice in Chapter 3 to visit companies who are doing a good job in quality, and have everyone visit to see firsthand what a quality organization looks like.

You need to feed people continuously with videos of companies that are doing a good job in quality.

Identify areas in every department and in every individual's job where they are doing a good job in quality.

Explain that your journey is going to mean making these good practices the norm and not the exception.

Make the picture very tangible and very concrete.

In the preface, I talked about the values I was given by my mother and father. You too were given a basic set of values as a child. If your company is going to be operating in a quality manner, you need to have everyone agree on these basic values, or principles.

That basic set of values will become the "ten commandments" of your new organization. Philip Crosby did an excellent job in this regard with his Four Absolutes of Quality. You must write down your values, just as Moses received the Ten Commandments on stone tablets.

Thomas Watson, Sr., gave IBM "respect for the individual, best possible service to our customer, and every task performed in a superior manner." Until you and your senior managers practice your values all day, every day, then the rest of the organization won't even be interested. When you were a child, you tried to do what your parents said, but subconsciously you always copied their actions and not their words.

As the organization changes to being more customer-focused, the structure of the organization will also change, becoming flatter, and people's roles will change. The president may become more operational, and will no longer give approval to ship nonconforming goods, or give precedence to his (or her) favorite clients. The vice president may become more of a planner and less of a crisis manager. The supervisor will become more of a team player and less of a babysitter.

We will talk more about the shape and structure of the new organization later.

BARRIERS TO CHANGE

Let's look at some of the barriers to change that we actually build ourselves by misusing the tools and techniques of change. These barriers include our meetings, our education, and our administration, among other factors.

Meetings

I think the John Cleese video "Meetings, Bloody Meetings" should be required viewing for all who enter the quality improvement world. Time and again, people end up with a quality process that is an endless round of meetings. The more you talk about change, the less time you have to implement it. We'll discuss meetings more fully in the chapter on Teamwork, but for now, let's just be aware that they can be an even bigger time waster than they are already. Clear objectives, a specific agenda, and good preparation must keep meetings to a minimum frequency and a minimum duration.

Education

A lot of people in business love education, because as long as you keep *learning* new stuff, you don't have to go out and apply it. The other problem is that people go for education saturation, leaving everyone so totally absorbed with new knowledge that they don't know where to start applying it. "Just-in-time" education is the secret here. The half-life of education is about 30 days. In other words, if you haven't used your new knowledge within a month, then you lose half of it.

Bureaucracy

Making quality a series of manuals, documents, and minutes of meetings brings death by steady suffocation. This is partly the legacy of the old quality control approach, and partly a problem caused by big organizations, such as the large automobile and computer manufacturers. Such bureaucracy creates a barrier as impenetrable as the old Berlin Wall. Change can't happen without multilevel approval. The time required to write in change means that change is outdated before it is implemented.

We Can Do It Ourselves

Ultimately, you must make the change yourself, but you need help to show you how to do it and you need someone outside of your organization to kick you when you're in danger of becoming complacent. Everyone in your organization has a vested interest in the status quo; you cannot be a prophet in your own land. You must have someone who answers to no one in the organization to tell you where you are going adrift.

NATIONAL CULTURE

These are some of the most difficult barriers to overcome. They are often excuses to say, "We're different; these principles of quality don't apply to us…" The American approach to problems is often "ready, fire, aim." The national culture produces great people of action, but with a reluctance to plan and think ahead, which is clearly important behavior if you want to stop being reactive to the customer.

The British are preoccupied with debate, and punctuating every sentence to the last technical detail. These are important attributes when working up those "up-front" requirements, but there is a tendency to remain stuck in the mode and never act; in many ways, the reverse of the American approach.

Canadians always reckon they are a blend of British and American cultures, but this isn't all good news. Canadians have great respect for the individual, which is a tremendous asset to build into your company culture, but the "Canadian Book of Service Excellence" is sadly one of the shortest volumes in the world. A visit to McDonald's north and south of the Canada/U.S. border will show you this difference in national culture.

You are not stuck with your national culture when it comes to building your company culture. Recognize the strengths in your national culture, and build on them. Identify the weaknesses, and deal with them.

THE STRESS OF CHANGE

You can't avoid stress. Change is stressful, and stress is another barrier that must be confronted. When we look in detail at the change process, we will see how breaking change into bite-size chunks, involving everyone (no secrets), and having a clearly shared vision are some of the ways to deal with this stress.

Change is not a "one-shot" activity. You either keep changing or die. You have to decide whether you are going to keep steering toward the vision you have designed (and this will constantly grow and change), or whether you are going to let the seven seas of the business world push you on a random course toward what might be storm and tempest, hidden rocks, or the Sargasso Sea. Better to take steps to deal with the stress of the change you choose than to allow random destruction through forces you can't control.

THE TIME TO INVEST IN CHANGE

I repeatedly find people who are trying to get started in quality and just cannot find the time that is needed to manage the quality process and work on eliminating problems. I'm often as guilty as they are. There is always a customer we must respond to, but unless we devote time to improving our own health and the health of our organizations, both will deteriorate.

Budget Time for Quality

Successful Japanese companies devote 15 percent of their time—nearly one day a week—to continuous improvement. When you carry out that first cut cost of quality (see Chapter 12), you'll find you waste at least 25 percent of your time reworking information, fire fighting, or dealing with unhappy customers. You must, must, *must* budget time for quality. Start with two hours a week minimum, but four hours a week is better, and that is less than 10 percent of your time! But you must give that time every week. In Chapter 9, I will ask you to identify how you spend your time. You'll need to sacrifice something in that list to create those four hours. And be realistic about your sacrifice. You will not fit those extra four hours in your lunch hour or after hours. You must be talking prime time for quality improvement activity.

Decide How to Spend That Time

Next you need to decide how you will spend that time:

- You'll probably have an hour a week initially (an hour every two weeks later on) with the quality management team.

- You'll need an hour a week working with your department on process improvement in the department, and probably an hour a week on one of the cross-functional corrective action teams.

- Finally, give an hour a week to yourself on process improvement in your own job or increasing your personal skills and knowledge of quality.

These are only suggestions. You might well allocate your time differently, but you must at least allocate time to the categories I've described, and I strongly suggest you keep a daily check sheet of the time you spend on quality.

If this all sounds familiar, then you've probably taken a time management course at some time in the past. If you haven't, then I suggest you do so at some time in the very near future.

It all comes down to being as disciplined about how you allocate your time as you are with your money, and recognizing that you have to invest time in quality in order to get a return in quality.

Make Time for Education

Another big "time problem" arises when people start their education in quality. They see this education as a real infringement on time they could be spending fighting fires. They can't wait for the formal education to finish so they can get back to the mess they like to wallow in.

I talk about education in Chapter 14, but the key point with education and time is that once you or your staff have started investing, say, two hours a week in education, you commit to investing time in quality improvement once the formal education has finished.

Your time investment in continuous improvement must be forever.

Sun Tzu said in his book *The Art of War* that "The warrior who knows his enemy best will win the battle." Knowing the enemies of change will be one of your keys to success before embarking on the change process, which we will discuss in the next chapter.

Figure 6-1 shows a simple questionnaire to help you assess your own capacity to change.

How Do We Handle Change?

	Strongly Agree	Agree	Disagree	Strongly Disagree
1. We use customer feedback as a high-value information.	☐	☐	☐	☐
2. We ask our suppliers for feedback.	☐	☐	☐	☐
3. We accept our colleagues' ideas.	☐	☐	☐	☐
4. Everyone has two jobs: doing their job and improving their job.	☐	☐	☐	☐
5. Failure is not criticized.	☐	☐	☐	☐
6. We educate our people continuously.	☐	☐	☐	☐
7. We don't dwell on "the way we were."	☐	☐	☐	☐
8. We know what our organization intends to be like in three years.	☐	☐	☐	☐

Boxes Checked:				
Weighing Factor:	x4	x3	x2	x1
Subtotals:				

Now add your total score: _____

Now multiply by 3 = _____

The maximum possible score is 96. If you score more than 70 you are probably handling change well. Below 70 you should pick your 2 or 3 lowest score items and focus on these for action.

This exercise gives its best results when done by your workteam.

Figure 6-1. Change Management Questionnaire

BROWSER'S BRIEFING

- When you initiate a culture change, people will be scared, even when the change seems to benefit them.
- Business leaders are role models for the new culture, both in the way they act as individuals and in their behavior with each other.
- Everyone needs to know where they are heading during this culture change, and why they are heading there.
- Middle managers and first-line supervisors are the most threatened by change. Their traditional role (and perhaps their job) is likely to be eliminated.
- A quality culture does not have a need for babysitters. You don't need people checking on other people to see if they did it right the first time.
- People like change. People don't like *being* changed.
- Senior managers who have skills as crisis managers will not need those skills in a quality culture.
- A clear vision is a prime requirement for overcoming resistance to change.
- The vision has to be based on agreed upon values.
- Meetings can be a barrier to change. The more you talk, the less you actually act.
- Education can be a barrier to change. As long as you stay in education mode, you don't need to act.
- New paperwork can clog the arteries of the organization, and can be a barrier to change.
- Fooling yourself that you can do it by yourself is a great way to get stuck in an organizational logjam.
- Saying that your national culture is not appropriate to a quality company culture is admitting defeat.
- Change creates stress in the organization and in its individuals. You need a plan to deal with the stress and eliminate it.
- Change takes time. The organization and the people need a time budget in the same way you need a cash budget. Plan your time and use the time you plan.

7 | The Change Process

Elton Mayo is a name familiar to those who have studied behavioral sciences. He is best known for the Hawthorne experiments, conducted at the Western Electric plant near Chicago in the late 1920s. The part of his work that is most celebrated was a series of tests he did on the effect of lighting intensity on the productivity of employees. As he increased the lighting in a work area, he measured and found an increase in the productivity of those employees.

Unremarkable, you might say. If I can see better, of *course* I can work better. The twist came when, good scientist that he was, Mayo carried out a control experiment. He dropped the lighting level, just to confirm that productivity would decrease. To his surprise, productivity *increased*. The increase occurred because attention was given to the people, and not because of the increased lighting. He unearthed the important "people" element in productivity during the mechanistic times of work study; a time when people's identities were being removed from their daily working lives.

At about the same time, Walter Shewhart was developing his ideas on process analysis and statistical process control. He saw the importance of measuring the performance of a process and analyzing the data in order to pinpoint weaknesses in the process. He showed that people were often asked to produce results from a process that was incapable of providing those results, and no amount of effort would overcome the process limitation. The importance of measurement in driving improvement was uncovered by Shewhart.

JURAN'S AND DEMING'S INSIGHTS

Two more people enter the story here, the two great gurus of quality, W. Edwards Deming and Joseph Juran. Both had the good fortune to work at the Hawthorne plant at that same time. They saw the importance of achieving a balance between process and people, when you are looking for improvement in the quality of your goods or services.

So many over the years have ignored this fundamental truth. I have seen organizations which believe that process management or statistical process control is all that is needed to root out problems. They have totally ignored the need to build trust and teamwork through improvements in interpersonal communication skills, and the need to give people feedback and recognition.

Equally, I have seen organizations invest heavily in team building and communication workshops and develop wonderful reward systems, but totally lack any numbers as evidence of change or improvement. Everyone says how wonderful the work environment has become, but ask them for hard evidence of happier customers and they shrug.

In the 1980s, before the crash of 1987, many companies invested in an "enlightened" fashion in the soft skills, the people improvement skills. As the recession of the 1990s bit deeper, companies invested less in their people, and looked for instant results from process management.

The balance between people and process during change is critical. You must not engage in process improvement activity without dealing with people improvement at the same time.

A MODEL FOR CHANGE

Change must be led from the top of the organization. Change will involve processes and people, and change will be continuous if you want to deliver quality services and quality products to your customer. I find the model diagram in Figure 7-1 helps people remember the key components. We will come back to the leadership issue in Chapters 8 and 9, and will focus on maintaining continuity in Chapter 18. In this chapter we focus on the issues of people and process in the change model. These two arms of the model are often referred to as the "hard skills" (process)

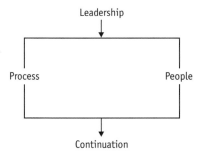

Figure 7-1. Key Components of Change

and "soft skills" (people) of quality. The process improvement arm of quality deals with the analytic and numerical side of quality improvement, while the people improvement arm deals with the creative and developmental side. You could call them the left brain and right brain of quality improvement.

Developing the change model further, Figure 7-2 shows four stages within each arm. The four stages are quite arbitrary. There could be ten stages in each arm, but I find most people are comfortable considering four. It's a bit like saying that science comprises mathematics, physics, chemistry, and biology. We know there are many more divisions, but these four are convenient as working divisions.

Focusing on Process Improvement

The four stages of process improvement are developed in Chapters 10 through 13. You will follow these stages over a period of many months as you seek to improve your processes, or you may at times fast-track the sequence in one day in order to tackle a specific problem.

Process Ownership

The first activity that is overlooked by so many who have entered the quality arena is to establish *process ownership*. This has to be done, first at the business level, and then down into the departmental and operational levels (see Figure 7-3). In doing this, you will unearth many "orphaned"

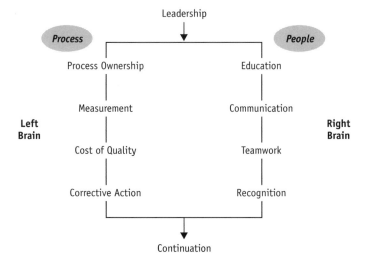

Figure 7-2. Process Improvement Model

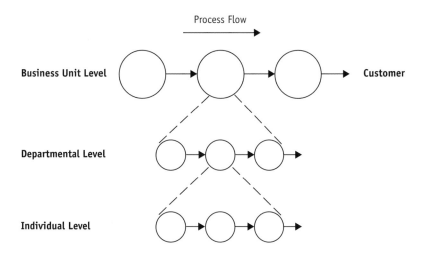

Figure 7-3. Process Ownership Model

processes, and just assigning owners will produce dramatic improvements. You may find over half your processes lack *clear* ownership.

Measurement

Process owners can then start agreeing on requirements with their internal customers and suppliers, and flushing out the requirements that are not being met. These nonconforming requirements can then be measured. Too often, I see companies that start measurement without doing the critical foundation work of process ownership. *Measurement* must be done by the owner of the process, who may well need the support of the internal customer in collecting measurement data. This is where we see the importance of the soft skills in "enabling" the communication here to work freely and to cut out finger-pointing.

Cost of Quality

Measurement data will cause process owners to think about the root cause of the process problems, and we will see in Chapter 11 how measurement is the cutting edge of process improvement. Measurement data tells us the magnitude of the process problems, and this is where the wonderful tool of *cost of quality* comes into play. The great advocates of cost of quality have been Philip Crosby and Joseph Juran, and in Chapter 12 we will explore cost of quality in depth. Cost of quality enables you to translate your measurement data into the common language of business, and so to prioritize which process problems should be the focus of your very finite business resources. Cost of quality enables you to translate your measurement data into the common language of business, and so to prioritize which process problems should be the focus of your very finite business resources. Cost of quality also enables you to measure return on investment for your improvement efforts. In short, cost of quality is the language of business, and it is also a communications tool.

Corrective Action

You will have applied *corrective action* to many of your problems as you go through previous stages of process improvement, and you will then be left with a core of problems that typically run across the different functions of your organization. This is where a systemized approach to corrective action will be needed. Using cost of quality to drive your corrective action system will make it operate much more easily, and at the end of a corrective action project, the team that tackled a problem will see the dollar reward for their effort.

Focusing on People Improvement

The four stages of people improvement will be discussed in detail in Chapters 14 through 17. The following sections introduce each stage briefly.

Education

Clearly, the first step in people improvement must be *education*. This seems a costly item, but to quote a T-shirt logo, *"If you think education is expensive, try ignorance."* Education feeds into and links with all the other steps in the change process. Education is vital before people can even participate effectively in the process improvement arm of the change process.

Education can also be one of the biggest barriers to change. I mentioned in Chapter 6 that people love to get trapped in education, because it means they don't have to go and do anything. You should provide just-in-time education, so people can learn a bit and do a bit. Good time planning for this and all other parts of the change process is important.

Communication

Education will launch the other stages of the people arm of the change process, and in particular, *communication*. Poor interpersonal communication is one of the major obstacles to delivering quality. Amazingly, Albert Mehebrian found that over 80 percent of communication is neither written nor spoken. The majority of our communication occurs through body language in the form of signs and signals. In addition, even the smallest organization needs a communication system that functions across all levels, and techniques like team briefing will help here. As your organization becomes more customer-focused, then horizontal communication becomes more important than vertical communication. Communication skills are vitally important in the transactions between internal customers and suppliers, and most of all with your external customer.

Teamwork

As your internal communications improve, and as you develop your internal customer/supplier linkages, you'll find people operating in natural work groups, or teams, and *teamwork* skills will need development. You will find this activity links very strongly with the leadership step. As more teams develop, more leaders are needed, and more training in leadership is required. The lack of team leadership skills is another of the hidden barriers to the smooth operation of the change process. Many people are discovering the need to invest in leadership training across all levels of the organization, and are also finding the nature of leadership is changing as they move to self-managed teams. Two years into the quality improvement process the general manager of Ontario Hydro's Pickering facility recognized the need for further investment in leadership training as their teamwork developed. The corrective action step also links up with teamwork when you start to set up teams to tackle cross-functional problems in your organization. Corrective action teams will bring together people who have never worked together before, and good teamwork skills will be vital for efficient operation.

Recognition

The fourth stage in the people arm of the change process is *recognition*. You will find this to be one of the most talked about, widely used, but least understood and least effectively implemented activities in the change process. People will feel insecure as change progresses. As they become more preventive and less reactive, a small voice inside them will say, "But I always got rewarded in the past for being reactive and being good in a crisis." If you want to encourage new behaviors, you must be clear on which ones to encourage, and then relentlessly reward and recognize these new behaviors. Only then will you banish the insecurity and reluctance to change. Rewarding and recognizing prevention will not come easily. You'll probably also find the need for a complete redesign of your payment and salary system.

THE BALANCE OF HARD AND SOFT SKILLS

Earlier in this chapter, I mentioned how W. Edwards Deming had been fortunate to be a student of both Mayo (soft skills) and Shewhart (hard skills). This is necessarily a simplification of the full story, but it is worth closing this chapter by relating subsequent events.

Through World War II, Deming became involved in the U.S. Census Bureau because of his statistical skills. The end of the war saw Europe and the Far East an economic ruin, and North America with the world's only truly intact economy. Deming talked about his beliefs in quality improvement, as did Joseph Juran. But North America had no need to listen; they could sell everything they made, and quality was all but irrelevant.

Deming went to Japan on postwar census activity, and caught the attention of Ichiro Ishikawa, one of the leaders of Japanese business. Deming addressed a now-famous dinner meeting in 1951, and lit the fire of Japanese economic revival through quality. The Japanese began to blend hard and soft skills, and the rest is history. Between 1950 and 1980, the world market share of U.S. auto manufacturers fell from 76 percent to 23 percent. American electronics goods manufacturers declined in domestic market share from 96 percent to less than 1 percent between 1955 and 1975, and even in a new high-tech industry like microchips, the U.S. share fell from 60 percent to 40 percent during the 1980s (Bowles and Hammond 1991).

In 1981 American television screened a program about this Japanese success; North America finally began to wake up. The third guru of quality had what the others lacked: timing and packaging. Between 1980 and

1990, when he finally retired, Philip Crosby launched a thousand companies on his 14-step quality improvement process. His big break came through knowing Paul Rizzo at IBM, who gave him his first major opportunity.

Deming preached his 14 Points, and Juran promoted his Quality Trilogy. Each approach had different strengths, and different organizations gradually blended the teachings of these gurus to develop an approach to total quality management that filled their own specific needs.

Unfortunately, many companies used this tailoring approach to cut out some of the truths of TQM that they found difficult to accept. Others misunderstood the teachings of these early pioneers, and the basic message was often misinterpreted. Most frequently, companies tried to do in 30 months what had taken the Japanese 30 years. They simply picked up the tools of quality, but had not put in place the vital foundation work.

In the rest of this part we will look at how to manage the change process using the ten steps in the process model. We will see where people misunderstood or chose to ignore the truth of what was needed. As you analyze your own approach to quality, identify which things you should do differently so that you can do it right the second time.

BROWSER'S BRIEFING

- Improvement in the way an organization operates means change.
- There must be balance between people improvement and process improvement when you change the organization.
- Change must be led from the front of the organization, but everyone must be involved in the process. And the change must be continuous.
- *Process improvement* starts with defining the processess of the business, measuring their performance, selecting the poor performers, and then applying corrective action to those poor performers.
- *People improvement* starts with education of the individual and leads to improved interpersonal communication and better teamwork.
- People need feedback in both their process improvement and self-improvement, and recognition of new behaviors is key feedback.
- Process ownership activity will reveal which business activities are neglected, or even "orphaned." It should start at the business level, and work down to the individual level.
- Measurement must be done by the process owner, and is the cutting edge of change and process improvement.
- Cost of quality enables processes requiring attention to be prioritized, and success in improvement to be measured in the language of business (dollars).
- Corrective action should be applied in a structured manner, using a corrective action system and the tools of problem solving.
- Education and training are what will ultimately differentiate you from other organizations. Don't waste education. Do it "just-in-time."
- Communication problems are the biggest cause of organizational failure. Invest in communication systems, and teach communication skills.
- Good teamwork is the outcome of people improvement. This is the core requirement for a smooth operation.

BROWSER'S BRIEFING

- Recognition gives people the feedback they need to ensure new behaviors are endorsed.
- The whole process is continuous and constantly recycled.
- The gurus (Deming, Juran, and Crosby) have different approaches, and we should learn from each of them.
- Your own quality improvement process must fit your own needs, but don't use this as an excuse to cut out fundamental truths.

8 | The Quality Management Team: Agents for Change

The management team is the primary agent for change, and yet all too often, it doesn't know what to do. I want to take you back to one early February in Canada. This usually means snow and subzero temperatures. The environment in the conference room at Nacan, a division of National Starch Company, was far from cool. A group of senior managers had been meeting for nearly four days and had been learning, debating, and analyzing how they would become the new team that would manage the quality improvement process at Nacan.

The company had been developing and implementing their quality process for a little over two years and the new team was excited at the challenges ahead. The old team had been led by the vice president of manufacturing, Brian Sayer, who was now company president. Sayer is a blunt, straight-talking Canadian from the north of England. His team had put quality values in place at Nacan and the commitment of his team had been unwavering. The new team had moved beyond this and was looking at the question, "How would I like my boss to show commitment and improvement in quality?" They listed specific actions, not generic clauses:

1. Spend real time with me and discuss quality issues.

2. Give me the time to invest in quality improvement.

3. Be a member of a corrective action team.

4. Support me when I make a decision.

5. Encourage me to obtain education and training.

6. Recognize me when I do a quality job.

7. Walk the talk.

At the end of the discussion one member of this new team said, "You know, that's exactly what my own people expect of me." They had realized that lack of quality or failure in quality was not something to blame on others. Although we are always talking about organizations, these organizations are made up of individuals. Quality is something for which we are all personally responsible. The other main lesson this team learned over the four days was that quality improvement is continuous—you don't give up after two years if you haven't delivered on all of your objectives. Their predecessors had worked hard and succeeded in developing a set of quality values. They now needed to move to the next step and take the baton from the team led by Brian Sayer.

Now let's move further back in time.

THE FINANCIAL ANALOGY

Back in the 1940s, Joseph Juran, one of the early gurus of quality, was having a real problem explaining to management teams their role in managing quality. He found them repeatedly wanting to be corrective action teams or debating societies. He coined the analogy, *"You manage quality in the same way you manage finances."*

If you are looking at a new business, your first activity in financial management is to analyze the book of accounts. This is analogous to the assessment activity we mentioned in Chapter 1. In financial management, we then draw up a plan for financial activity in the business over the next 12 months, and call it a budget. In quality management, preparing the 12-month plan is a job for the quality management team (QMT), and once the activities in the change process are understood, this becomes top priority. (We'll pursue this further in Chapter 18.) Figure 8-1 shows an example of a 12-month plan.

So far, so good, and most teams do fine up to this point. The next stage is where many go wrong. Each member of the management team

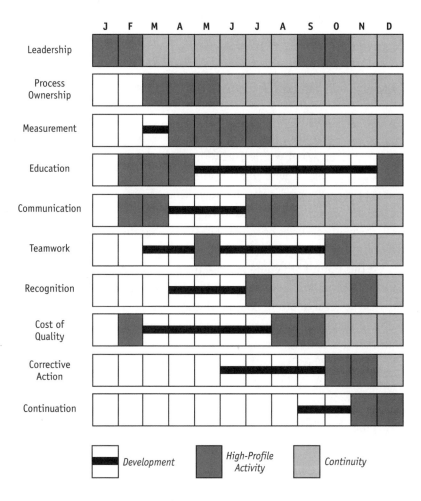

Figure 8-1. Implementation Timeline

has the job of implementing the quality plan in their own part of the business.

IMPLEMENTING THE QUALITY PLAN

Just as the sales manager is responsible for implementing the sales budget through the sales force or the research manager, the research budget through the research team, each member of the management team must implement quality activities like measurement, education, and recognition in their own function or department.

Depth and Span of Communication

The first organizational step in leading quality, and the next place where people go wrong, is in the role and structure of the management team. Have you ever asked yourself why the ideal size of a business unit is about 250 people or why you run into communication problems once you get over 300 people? We all know the ideal span of control is about six people; organizations have shown this for thousands of years. Just go back through centuries of military history if you think otherwise. What we hear far less about is the ideal *depth* of control.

At this point I am going to erase the word *control* with all its implications of command and power, and replace it with the word *communication*. The ideal depth of communication is three layers; combine this with the ideal span of communication of six people and you have a general manager with six heads for each of the main business functions. These function heads each have six managers, who in turn manage six staff. Add this up and you get 259 people (see Figure 8-2).

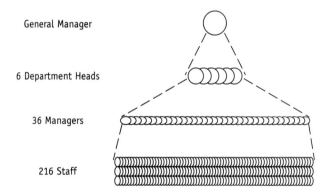

General Manager

6 Department Heads

36 Managers

216 Staff

Figure 8-2. Ideal Depth and Span of Organizational Communication

I can hear you say, "We're not like that." "We're different." "Two of our departments have two layers, and finance has only six people." I'm talking in broad terms, and if you think about it, the evidence is over-whelming. Once you try to communicate through more than three layers, the message gets lost. Once an organization grows much over 300 people it starts to split like an amoeba. Even if the split is not official, it has probably happened informally. Alternatively, anarchy sets in.

Think of all the work that organizations are doing to flatten them-selves. Finally, as you get deeper into analyzing your business processes, you'll see that by simplifying the process flow of your business, you will require no more than three layers. I've worked with so many organiza-tions, every one of which is different, and yet the maximum effective size of the business unit is nearly always 30 to 50 managers and 150 to 200 staff.

You might be wondering about network management and empower-ment, and yes, these are natural developments as organizations become more self-confident and develop their own self-esteem. You can't use these as techniques to effect change, however; they are the *results* of successful change in a quality organization. In fact, Chapter 22 looks at the way your organizational structure will develop as you become more customer-focused.

Empowerment is the next point at which you may have gone wrong. You set up your quality management team as the agent for change, and decided to empower people by putting all the believers on the team. The problem is that the "believers," in spite of their commitment to the "new religion" of quality, are not able to implement change. The believers might have come from the middle or lower points of the organization and found themselves working without authority against the vested interest of their bosses, who have probably said, "We tried that before and it didn't work."

The quality management team is the primary agent for change and must consist of the six or seven people who lead the business unit. These people have the job of planning the change process, and they each also have the job of making the change happen in their own department.

HOW TO SUPPORT
IMPLEMENTATION OF THE PLAN

To implement change, the management team must act in unison, and each function head will need support in implementation.

You create this support by having each team member become a specialist in one, or perhaps two, elements in the change process. One of you will be the education specialist, another the measurement champion, another will coordinate the corrective action system, and so on.

How will this work? Let's assume that you've reached the point on your timeline where the management team wants to implement measurement. (Look at the timeline in Figure 8-1.)

You agree that between now and your next team meeting, each team member is going to ensure that each process owner in their department has identified the main nonconformance to be measured, set up a chart, and started collecting data. *The department head, not the measurement champion, is responsible to see that this happens.*

The measurement champion gives support by providing company measurement charts, answering questions on measurement technique, and providing any resources the department might need to carry out measurement. The measurement champion also ensures that each function head has kept their promise of implementing measurement in their own department.

Conducting QMT Meetings

When the quality management team meets again, the chairperson will include on the agenda "Progress on Initiating Measurement." Each function head will report, *in two minutes or less*, their progress and any problems they are experiencing, and the measurement champion will summarize strengths and weaknesses and identify actions to be taken. If any function heads are having problems, the champion will work with them between meetings. The whole agenda item on measurement will take 15 to 20 minutes, and will *not* arise at every QMT meeting.

Measurement will only be discussed when it is in its "high profile" phase in the quality plan.

The magic ingredient to keep the action moving forward at QMT meetings is *peer pressure*. If you yourself have implemented measurement, and another team member hasn't, both you and your colleagues want to know why they're letting the team down. It mustn't be just the measurement team champion or chairperson who exerts this pressure. We'll be looking in more detail at teamwork skills in Chapter 16.

Summarizing this modus operandi for the quality management team, you will:

- Plan it as a team.

- Implement it in the department and

- Advance it as a team. (see Figure 8-3)

The QMT meetings should be held monthly, although you may have them every two weeks in the early stages of your quality process. They should be run in the same way as you run the financial review of the business. There should be a review of the month's activity as I described the review of measurement. You identify any variations from the plan, and make quick decisions on actions to deal with the variances. The minutes of the meeting should only list decisions and actions with persons responsible.

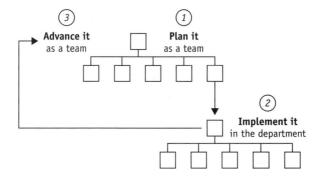

Figure 8-3. Quality Management Team (QMT) Process

If your management review is taking more than an hour, then chances are you're getting into problem solving. *Problem solving is not the responsibility of the quality management team.* Problems either relate to the operation of the change process, in which case they are the responsibility of the step champion, or they relate to the business processes, in which case they are the responsibility of the function head. Either of these people may request help in dealing with a problem, but the problem should be tackled outside of the QMT meeting.

Time and again I've seen management teams get sucked into brainstorming a corrective action on late delivery or staff shortage or paperwork difficulties. This is not the role of the QMT. These problems should be tackled, between meetings, by the people concerned.

As you see the role of the QMT unfold, you can see why it is essential that the team contains the key players in the business unit if you are going to effect change.

Each of these key players must be a personal agent for change, and each of them must have committed totally to the vision and values of the organization. The best way to show this commitment is to have seen each team member (not just the chief executive) sign the policy statement of your basic values and commitment to quality and the customer.

The other document I strongly recommend for this team is a "roles and responsibilities" document (a team job description), which again is signed by each team member. This document will look something like the example in Figure 8-4.

One agenda item I personally abhor is "Any other business." This is a license for anarchy, and for throwing your meeting process totally out of control. The chair should ask for any late agenda items at the start of the meeting, and unless something unusual has occurred, these should have been identified three days previously. In the event of the exceptional item, the team should agree whether to extend the meeting, hold over the item until the next meeting, or insert the item in place of something else on the agenda.

You may have noticed in Figure 8-4 a person described as the administrator. This person will be responsible for the agenda and minutes, but will not be a secretary or typist. This is the person next to the president or chief executive who will be the prime advocate of quality in the organization. The ISO 9000 standards call for a "management-appointed representative." In larger organizations, this may be the director or vice president of quality, or the quality coordinator. Between meetings of the QMT, the administrator must constantly be feeling the quality pulse of the organization, and must work closely with the leader of the organization in assessing the achievement of the quality objectives of your organization. Don't make the mistake of choosing an administrator who has no clout. If you make this mistake, the poor administrator will get blamed for all your failures, and will have no authority in the eyes of the rest of the team.

Quality Management Team Roles and Responsibilities
(Norton Engineering—Windsor Site)

1. To plan, implement, and monitor total quality management at the Windsor Site of Norton Engineering.

2. Chairperson (and Leadership Champion) —   *Charles Pearson*
   Administrator (and Continuation Champion) —   *Ada Minton*
   Process Ownership and Measurement Champion —   *Wendel Gilmore*
   Cost of Quality and Corrective Action Champion —   *Mallory Knox*
   Education and Recognition Champion —   *Randall McMurphy*
   Communication and Teamwork Champion —   *Frank Booth*

3. The team will meet on the first Tuesday of each month at 9:00 a.m. in the company conference room. Meetings will be designed to last one hour.

4. The meeting agenda will be issued a minimum of three (3) days before the meeting. Agenda items should be submitted a minimum of five (5) days before the meeting.

5. Minutes will be issued again within 48 hours of a meeting, and will list decisions from the meeting, and subsequent actions, with persons responsible.

Signed,   _____

             _____

             _____

             _____

             _____

             _____

Figure 8-4. A Team "Job Description"

SETTING THE STANDARD

Finally, the reminder, if you haven't already guessed it. The quality management team will be the role model for quality practices in your organization. The way you run your QMT will set the standard for all the other teams and individuals in your organization. We'll talk about teamwork in Chapter 16, and we'll be talking about leadership and role modeling in the next chapter. The QMT is in the fishbowl. Start on time, finish on time, stick to the agenda, and *tell* the rest of the people about your meetings, don't just post the minutes.

All through this chapter, as we've talked about teamwork, there has been an underlying implication of leadership. In Chapter 9, we'll look at the issue of leadership, and what our personal role must be in leading the change to a quality and customer-focused organization.

BROWSER'S BRIEFING

- The management team is the primary agent for change in the organization.
- The management team must be clear in its role as a change agent.
- Quality must be managed, just as you manage your finances.
- The management team must build a detailed plan for implementing change to a quality organization.
- Each member of the team is responsible for implementing the plan in their own areas of the business.
- The change management team should only try to implement change in an area of no more than 300 people.
- The management team must include the key people who lead the business unit.
- The business leaders cannot immediately become experts in all aspects of change management. Each should specialize, or champion, one or two elements of the change process, e.g., *measurement* plus *cost of quality*, or *education*, or *teamwork* plus *recognition*.
- A specialist in, say, measurement would be available to his or her colleagues for advice on an as-needed basis.
- A specialist would be responsible for monitoring their element of the change process, which is being implemented throughout the business. But the department heads make it happen.
- The quality management team must plan change, implement it, and advance it.
- The QMT meets monthly to review progress. Problem solving is done offline between meetings.
- The QMT is the role model for change in the organization. Each member of the team will also be leading change in their part of the organization.

9 Leadership

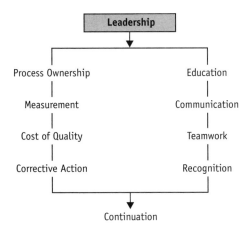

You've probably heard about the difference between leadership involvement and leadership commitment. It's a story about "ham and eggs."

A hen and a pig lived on a farm and the farmer was a really caring person who looked after their every need. They decided that they wanted to thank the farmer for all this care and attention. After some discussion, they decided they would cook him a meal, to which they would each make their own special contribution. The farmer's favorite meal was breakfast, and so they finally agreed that they would cook the farmer a meal of ham and eggs. There was a short pause after they had finally arrived at agreement, and the pig looked a bit concerned. The pig then said to the chicken, "Hey, you may be involved in this, but me, I'm committed!"

The hen is involved; the pig is committed. The people around you can see very quickly whether you are involved or committed, and leadership can be an apparently thankless and also very demanding activity.

In the 1960s, Norman Maier did extensive research on team success. He concluded, "The primary determinant of a team's success is the skill of the person leading it." Many centuries before this, in a very different part of the world, Lao-Tzu concluded, "When the best leader's work is done, the people say, 'We did this work ourselves.'"

If you're looking for the reason why the team you lead isn't succeeding, then look no further than yourself. However, if your team is successful then you can expect them to take the credit. I'm going to add a third saying, familiar to us all, which is going to be the theme of this chapter, and that is: *Actions speak louder than words.*

Unless you personally practice quality in all your day-to-day activities, the employees will see right through you. People will notice your actions, not your wonderful words. You may be making incredible insightful strategic decisions and risking your own skin for the future of the business, but very few people see this. It's your own day-to-day activities that impact people around you far more than you realize. It's how you run your meetings, conduct your interviews, and write your reports that tells people whether you really believe, deep down, in the basic principles of quality.

This all makes leadership sound like a very thankless task, and yet we're all faced with leading at some time in our lives. The task doesn't always just fall to the company president. In the world of quality improvement, people see the need for better leadership and teamwork in order for an organization to run smoothly. People also see repeated failure in quality improvement due to poor teamwork, which is caused by poor leadership.

A leader has to get agreement on where the team is heading. You must define the team's principal objective, whether it is to win a football game or to assemble televisions. In addition, your objective in leading quality in your team will be to work to continuously improve your processes. You then find you are better positioned to deal with those customer requirements that change in the future, because your team processes have become leaner and more responsive. However, many teams go wrong by not defining their objectives in a language the whole team can understand, and in thinking that agreed upon objectives are *all* the team needs! In this chapter I will focus on the values that you and the team use to build your objectives for the team, and hence your picture, or vision, of where the team is heading.

Leading a team requires something much deeper than agreed upon objectives. The Malcolm Baldrige National Quality Award criteria, for example, look for how the company's leadership "incorporates clear values, company directions, high performance expectations, a strong customer focus, and continuous learning" (1997 Baldrige Award Criteria).

TEAM VALUES

Every organization or team has to have a set of values or principles upon which everyone agrees. People can then start to agree on how they will achieve the team's objectives. We discussed values in Chapter 5, and it's important for a team and its leader to regularly reaffirm commitment to these basic values.

Have you and your team agreed on your definition of quality? This is your most basic value; quality is defined by the customer, and not by you. You will see later that this puts a big responsibility on the leader, to talk with internal and external customers and agree on customer requirements.

Having defined quality, how will you deliver it? Do you and your team check everything before you send information or materials to another department or another company? On the other hand, is it in your basic values that you will build prevention into your business processes, so that checking will become unnecessary? This is a deep-seated value that asks whether you are a forward thinker or a firefighter. I remember when as chief executive of a 300-person business, I was recruiting a lot of new staff. Peter Robinson, the CEO of a related company, commented that I should be careful not to recruit people who are good in a crisis. "It's surprising," he said, "how the best firefighters are often the arsonists." Ask yourself if you are subconsciously allowing crises to develop just to make yourself look good.

The only way to deliver quality effectively is through prevention, which means investing time in developing the skills of your team, ensuring you have the right equipment, and ensuring that all of your work processes have clear procedures. Procedures are usually the most neglected part of it all.

Breaking agreed upon procedures causes more chaos and wasted time in your team than you would ever realize, and yet the team leader is usually more guilty of this than any team member. Ask yourself if you are a role model or if you exert the "leader's privilege" and flaunt the rules.

Finally, ask yourself if you and your team work together to improve the service you give to the next department or the outside customer, or do you complain that there's nothing you can do about the problems being constantly dumped on you. Do you continue to insist that the customer is always changing their mind? When there's a problem, do you put in a quick fix which you're going to "come back to later"? On the other hand, do you hold the value that you will work continuously to meet all customer requirements? Do you have an attitude that no nonconformance is acceptable, and when nonconformance does occur, do you take preventive action to remove the root cause?

COMMUNICATING VALUES

Most leaders pride themselves on their communication skills, and yet so often this is their downfall. Look at the basic model in Figure 9-1. We communicate on three levels: verbally, visually, and with feelings. Most leaders think that their spoken or written communication is what really matters, but the big shock is that words, written or spoken, typically account for only about one-sixth (15 to 20 percent!) of our communication with others. As well, different cultures and individuals have different balances of these components. The British style of communication is more verbal; they wrap everything in words, whereas Americans are far more visual (a nation raised on TV and movies).

Do you know the type of communication needed inside your own team? Accountants may be verbal, designers visual, and perhaps your sales people communicate with feelings! Remember that actions

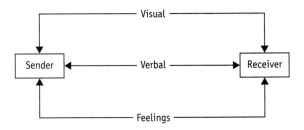

Figure 9-1. Levels of Communication

speak louder than words, and that you will communicate your commitment to the quality values of your team by what you do, and far less by what you say.

LEADERSHIP ACTIONS

What are the actions a good leader will take to communicate these quality values? Since 1983 James Kouzes and Barry Posner have collected data from thousands of leadership situations from all types of organizations. They have identified five "fundamental practices" successful leaders have in common:

- Challenging the process
- Inspiring a shared vision
- Enabling others to act
- Modeling the way
- Encouraging the heart (Kouzes and Posner 1995, 9)

Kouzes and Posner elaborate on these five fundamentals in an excellent book, *The Leadership Challenge,* now in its second edition. These basics will of course apply to leadership in the quality process.

At the top of the list is *challenging the process*—in other words, continuous process improvement! As you will see, this becomes the core activity of quality leadership, into which your other leadership actions are built. *Inspiring a shared vision* is related to the value work we discussed in Chapter 5. You have to create your objectives and build your vision by involving the whole team. This leads to *enabling others to act.*

If your team has participated in building the objectives, then they have ownership, but you must still give them the skills they need, as well as the equipment. (Remember prevention?)

Kouzes and Posner include *modeling the way* as a key practice of good leaders. Your participation is essential to the success of the change process. Remember, actions speak louder than words. This is where many leaders have a lot of difficulty. Maintaining the balance between being a thinker and a doer is tough. Most of us manage one or the other, but not both.

The challenging, the visioning, and the enabling were all about thinking and talking, but now you are being asked to *do* something! If you don't participate, your team is probably saying behind your back that you "talk a good game, but…" As you read you will see the importance of applying participation and modeling to your personal work processes as well as the teams' processes.

The last practice emphasized by Kouzes and Posner is *encouraging the heart*. A leader succeeds by creating enthusiasm in the organization. Communicating your feeling for the work is essential. Unless you believe in the values, vision, and objectives of the team, you won't fool anyone. The more deeply *you* believe in what the team is doing, the easier it is to spread your enthusiasm to the others.

Kouzes and Posner also researched the personal characteristics that constituents look for and admire in leaders. Since their research began, four qualities have consistently topped the list. Most people want leaders who are

- Honest
- Forward-looking
- Inspiring
- Competent (Kouzes and Posner 1995, 21)

It is interesting to look at this list in light of the 1996 U.S. presidential election, and to see how honesty, a forward vision, enthusiasm, and competence played key roles in the strategies of both candidates.

Remember how Bob Dole tried to attack Bill Clinton over honesty? Both candidates sought to impress the public with their vision of a better future, and different voters responded to these different visions. Both candidates showed strong enthusiasm, and Bob Dole's 96-hour marathon at the end of the campaign was remarkable. Bill Clinton had an ability to convey a sense of deep personal feelings about the issues and enthusiasm for the challenges of the future. In terms of competence, he had the advantage of having led the United States for the previous four years and the benefit of a strong economy during the campaign.

Now think about these attributes for yourself. Also remember those points about communication. If your team is saying that you only talk a good game, this strikes right at the heart of the first requirement, honesty. Your actions are what tell people whether you really believe what you are saying.

MEETINGS

The way you run your meetings has more impact on your team's effectiveness than most leaders realize. It's the way you show whether you really behave in accordance with your quality values. Who is the customer of the meeting process, the team leader or the team membership? Do you practice prevention in setting up your agenda, and do you continuously seek to improve the meeting process by using quality techniques, such as measurement?

The meeting is the focus of the team's identity. You must conform to customer requirements by not changing dates at the last minute, and by starting and finishing at the agreed time. Be preventive and issue the agenda at least three days before the meeting. I used to have a chairman who resolutely refused to bring an agenda when he visited my business. He always insisted that we "take it on the run." The result was that the executive team wasted one day times seven people preparing material for what was their best guess on the agenda content. The chairman would arrive, usually late, the team would arrive loaded with all the papers they thought were relevant, and he would spend half the meeting deciding what to talk about. Sound familiar? For your sake, I hope not.

THE TEAM'S CORE ACTIVITY

If you're going to show quality leadership to your team, then you and the team have to start applying continuous improvement to the processes that the team owns. Whether you are the sales team, the production team, or the design team, you need to identify which processes are your team's responsibility, and then work through the continuous improvement cycle, both as a team and as individuals.

Your first task in challenging the status quo of your team is to define who does what. To everyone's surprise, most processes on a team do not have clear ownership, and when you interface with other teams, you often find it's not clear which "team" is responsible for which process.

Unowned processes are one of the major causes of wasted time or materials for your team, and the team will thank you profoundly for helping sort this out inside your team, or between you and other teams.

Process ownership is discussed in detail in Chapter 10. Applying the technique inside your team will establish clear leadership.

When you start to work on your own work processes and eliminate your own wasted time and the wasted time of people around you, then you will start to convince people you are serious about quality and they will start to work on quality in the same way.

Build a flowchart for your own work processes and see which of the handoffs gives you the biggest problem or causes the most time-wasting. This is discussed in more detail in Chapter 10.

Nonconforming requirements provide the team leader with a real opportunity to participate in the improvement process by using measurement and showing actions do speak louder than words. One of the most common causes of failure in measurement is that leaders don't participate.

MEASUREMENT

Most leaders say that their own processes don't repeat often enough to make measurement meaningful. Sherritt Gordon, a precious metals company in Alberta, had this problem in choosing measurements. The vice president of quality, Dennis Maschmeyer, did a process analysis, and the executives started measuring items such as:

- Changes to meeting dates
- Late starts to meetings
- Changes in the business plan
- Problem-solving meetings due to unclear requirements
- Problem-solving visits to customers

None of these items are very complex, but all have a major impact on the achievement of quality for the organization. Most importantly, they also show leaders participating in the critical process of measurement.

I remember Bob Bayette, the quality manager of ICI Paints, telling me that the management team identified the process of their team meeting (and for that matter the whole company meeting process) as the greatest opportunity for improvement. Six months later, Bob said, they no longer had people arriving at meetings saying, "What's this meeting about?" They had measured the phenomenal amount of time people saved by controlling this process. I'll talk more about meetings in Chapter 16 and review the components that ICI worked on.

A measurement check sheet you can use looks something like Figure 9-2. You should keep it where you will be able to record nonconformances as they happen, whether that means by the phone, on the wall, or as a three-by-five-inch card in your pocket. Most importantly, let your team know you're doing it and have the courage to share your results. (Remember honesty!)

Most leaders don't know how they spend their time and don't know what their key tasks (key processes) are. Until you know these two things you don't know where to focus your own efforts for improving quality. Using the time log in Figure 9-3, go back through your day planner for the last 100 days. (You don't keep a day planner? And you expect other people to know how long it takes to do a job?)

Collect the seven major categories into which your time usage falls: internal meetings, customer meetings, product development, paperwork, customer phone calls, and so on. Beyond the seventh category will account for less than 5 percent of your time and your time usage is not

Problem Check Sheet					
	Monday	Tuesday	Wednesday	Thursday	Friday
Late to meetings	|	||			
Reschedule meetings		|	|		
Lost documents	|||				
Complaint visit		|	|		
Computer down					

Figure 9-2. A Simple Check Sheet for Tracking Problem Occurrences

Time Use			
Key Tasks	Hours/Week	Hours/Month	% of Time
1.			
2.			
3.			
4.			
5.			
6.			
7.			

Figure 9-3. A Log for Analyzing Time Use

significant (that doesn't mean the process is not significant!). The results may be surprising. If one of your significant processes accounts for less than 5 percent of your time, ask yourself if you have a problem.

Even if the results are what you expected, take the next step and chart the information requested in Figure 9-4. Who are the people you interact with? What do you do when you interact with them? What are your key activities? This is not easy, I know. You'll say that it changes every day and every week and every month. Until you can define these activities, however, you are not in control. You may want to start in the left column, the middle column, or the right column; it doesn't matter.

When you finally get your list, compare it with the list in the Figure 9-3 time log. Are you devoting the right amount of time to the right process? Reckon that a third of your time is wasted fire fighting or reprocessing information. Which of your time-wasting activities are you going to attack to cut out this waste? You can use the appproach described in Chapters 10 and 11 to show your own commitment or involvement in the quality improvement process.

Getting the team involved in measurement is the next step, and some of the members may be nervous thinking that you'll be checking out their shortcomings. Try measuring a process owned by all of the team to start with. I recall a sales office I worked with deciding on the five items that caused their biggest problem. They made up a white board for the office wall that looked like the check sheet in Figure 9-2.

Measurement of your own processes is the visual and practical way of showing an example to your team. If you do meaningful measurement on your personal work processes, they will follow your example.

HOW CAN I SHOW QUALITY LEADERSHIP TO MY TEAM?

What I'm talking about here is good old-fashioned self-improvement. Like it or not, you are a role model for the people around you. Whether you are 15, 35, or 65, if you are committed to quality, you will be working to improve your own work processes, and you'll be both measuring and displaying improvements to encourage people around you to work on improvements too.

Process (what we do)	Output (what we produce or deliver)	Delivered To (who we give our outputs to)
1. _____ _____		_____ _____
2. _____ _____		_____ _____
3. _____ _____		_____ _____
4. _____ _____		_____ _____
5. _____ _____		_____ _____
6. _____ _____		_____ _____

Figure 9-4. A Form for Surveying Internal Customers and Suppliers

At the outset, your team has to have a clear objective, or what some would call a mission, but the team has to agree on its basic values (call them "house rules") to achieve that objective. Using these values or principles, the team can then build a series of smaller objectives and develop its own vision of the larger objective.

All of this is "think and talk," and it is vital foundation work. However, too many leaders in business stay locked in this phase.

You communicate your true commitment to your team's objective of improving quality only when you are yourself working to improve quality. You have to participate in the analysis of your team process be it selling, manufacturing, or data processing. Delegation does not work. You have to work on your own part of the team process doing your own *meaningful* measurement.

You must have a clear idea of how you are going to spend or invest this time you are going to save; otherwise, you'll see no value in saving it. Will it be that exciting new product you want to work on but never get the time, will it be that market sector you want to attack but never get around to it, or will it be that filing system which is your next improvement project?

Use the following action list to get started in showing your personal commitment to improvement. In the chapters ahead, you will see how you can work on improvement of both processes and people for yourself and your organization.

1. Analyze your time use.

2. List your most important processes.

3. Identify transactions where time is wasted.

4. Flowchart your work processes.

5. Ask your internal customers how you waste their time.

6. Ask your internal suppliers how you waste their time.

7. Select a process you intend to improve.

8. Tell everyone what you intend to improve.

9. Tell yourself where you will spend the time you save.

10. Do it!

11. Measure your savings.

12. Move on to your next improvement project.

BROWSER'S BRIEFING

- The primary determinant of a team's success is the skill of the person leading it.
- When the best leader's work is done, the people say, "We did this work ourselves."
- People will do what you do, and not what you say.
- Leadership creates and sustains quality values.
- The leader's first task is to get the team to agree on its quality values and objectives.
- The leader communicates commitment to values through actions, not words.
- Successful leaders:
  - Challenge the process
  - Inspire a vision
  - Enable others to act
  - Model the way
  - Encourage the heart (Kouzes and Posner 1995)
- Followers looks for leaders who are:
  - Honest
  - Forward-looking
  - Inspiring (Kouzes and Posner 1995)
  - Competent
- Well-run meetings are one of the best gifts to give your team.
- Create an environment of continuous improvement for your team.
- Show your leadership example by personally conducting activities such as measurement.
- Remember, you are a role model, both in your good practices and your bad ones.

PART IV

THE PROCESSES

10 | Process Ownership

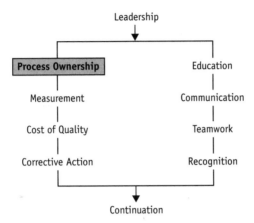

Scarborough, Ontario, was hit harder than most by the recession of the early 1990s. The Employment Canada office in Scarborough handles a stress level that few organizations could deal with. Can you imagine working in your own company with all of your own customers walking alongside you in the office corridor, and most of them are angry or upset because they have lost their job?

Against this background, Sondra Sullivan started her team on what today is fashionably called business reengineering. In 1991, they called it process management and still do. They used tools like process mapping and measurement to reduce the "cycle time" of desperately needed services to their clients. The approach was not complicated. They cataloged the business processes and the departmental processes, and then mapped these processes to show a process flow. The process owners in that organization now know who their internal customers and suppliers are, and have invested time and effort in finding the requirements of their customers. This has enabled them to focus on the requirements where problems exist and then work on eliminating those problems.

You've probably heard this famous saying, photocopied around offices worldwide:

> *There was an important job to be done, and Everybody was asked to do it. Everybody was sure Somebody would do it. Anybody could have done it, but Nobody did it. Somebody got angry about that because it was Everybody's job. Everybody thought Anybody could do it but Nobody realized that Everybody wouldn't do it. It ended up that Everybody blamed Somebody when Nobody did what Anybody could have done.*

Process ownership ensures that all people in the organization understand which processes are their responsibility, and who their customers and suppliers are.

BUILDING THE FOUNDATION

While many parts of quality are badly executed, I find process ownership the most overlooked. This is the tough and unexciting foundation work. I think again of building the extension to Hope Cottage in the early eighties. What kept me going was the vision created by the plans and drawings. I thought about the new room and how it would be decorated. I thought of the new view out toward the village church. I thought about the extra space my family would have to enjoy life together. As I worked, up to my knees in mud and clay, that vision kept me going. When you work on process ownership, you need to keep a clear vision of your company. You must maintain a clear vision for everyone, because process ownership work is not always exciting, but like the foundation of the house you live in, it is critical for supporting the rest of your work in quality.

Why is process ownership so important? Over half of the processes in your organization do not have clear ownership; without clear ownership, you don't have internal customers and suppliers talking to each other. If your customers and suppliers are not talking to each other, then they are not agreeing on requirements; and without agreed upon requirements, you cannot deliver quality.

Passing the Buck

The most frequent (and most disruptive) example of lack of process ownership that I encounter is an organization's photocopier. It is amazing the number of times I see the office staff nod and presidents blush when I say this.

In many companies, no one is responsible for ensuring the photocopier gets serviced, for ensuring the customers get what they require, or that the machine is capable of meeting those requirements. You might reply, "We have a service engineer we pay to do that." Not so: the engineer is an input to the process—not the process owner.

ESTABLISHING OWNERSHIP WITH PROCESS MAPPING

Mapping out a process for establishing ownership looks like this:

1. Identify customer and supplier functions.

2. Analyze time use.

3. Map the flow of business.

4. Establish ownership of unowned processes.

5. Agree on customer requirements.

6. Identify requirements not met.

7. Pinpoint communication flaws.

How do you begin process ownership? I start at the business unit level with a procedure called *process mapping*. Each function head has to identify the functions of their customers and suppliers. I also get these people to analyze their time use over the previous 100 days. Then I ask the questions, "Who are the people with whom you have the most important transactions?" and "Are you giving the right amount of time to the most critical processes?" This technique was described in Chapter 9 (see Figure 9-4 on page 110); it applies first at the business level and then at the department and work team level.

Go to 15 or 20 processes if you need to, and then compare your list with the time use log you completed in Chapter 9. Are you giving the right amount of time to the most critical processes? Who are the people with whom you have your most important transactions?

The next step is to map the flow of the business. You need to do this at the business level and keep it simple. An example of process flow at the business level is shown in Figure 10-1. You can apply it to almost any manufacturing or service business you could name. The emphasis will differ from business to business, and you will change some of the names, but use it as a guide to map the flow of your own business, and take some time to identify who owns which processes at the business level.

Once you have established ownership of your unowned processes, the new owners can then identify their customers and suppliers and start agreeing on requirements. The team leader should clearly both lead and participate in this activity, and the end product will be a series of requirements that are not being met by the team.

I like to use two or three flip charts with sticky notes to identify processes and process owners at the business level.

Now identify the transactions conducted between each of the process owners. Your wall now starts to look as if someone threw a plate of spaghetti at it! This tells you how much communication goes on, and also how much of it would be unnecessary if you did it right the first time.

That was the bad news. The even worse news is that you haven't reached the departmental level yet. It's not hard to see why poor communication is one of the biggest causes of poor quality.

So now what? You've got this huge spaghetti diagram on the wall, and everyone feels confused. There's a temptation among the more tenacious of us to analyze every process and every transaction, and try to boil the ocean. Don't.

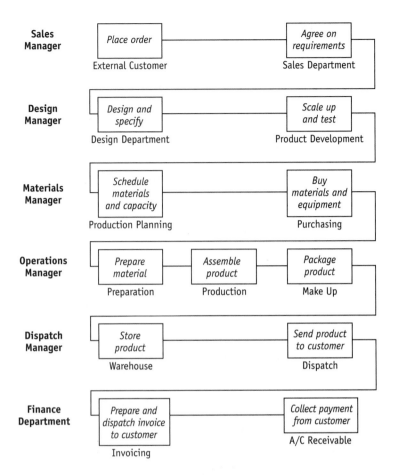

Figure 10-1. A Process Flow Map for a Business Unit

SURVEYING THE INTERNAL CUSTOMER

Each person in the organization needs to seek out their internal customer, and find out the following from each of them:

- Where do we not know your requirements?

- How do I cause you to waste time?

- When do I dump problems on you?

- When do I cause you hassles?

As soon as you read these questions, you see why company culture is going to determine the success or failure of this activity. Are people going to be open and free in their answers, or will they be abusive and defensive? I usually give an organization about a week to do this, and then I ask them, "Which of your internal suppliers (upstream processes) didn't approach you over the last week, but you wished they had because they are causing you problems?" I tell everyone to seek out those suppliers. This way, each person in the organization will have identified the main people they interact with, and the main ideas they can work on and improve.

The work so far has been revealing and interactive and fun. The next part is the boring, tough foundation work I warned you about.

MAPPING YOUR BUSINESS

In the months ahead, the people in the business need to be agreeing on requirements between their internal customers and suppliers. Each person should have a shopping list of people they will talk to. A form like the one in Figure 9-4 (page 110) can be used to guide their discussions.

Department managers should be guiding their staff people through these months of interaction. Each department should be building its own process map and identifying transactions that are weak or waste time. While this activity may not seem spectacular, you'll be making major strides as you agree on each set of requirements. You'll also see great opportunities to eliminate unnecessary or repetitive tasks and reduce the cycle time from customer order to customer delivery. One of the maps Employment Canada produced in their journey to reduce service cycle time is shown in Figure 10-2.

As you map your department or map your business, you will start to see why communication is such a problem in your organization. You must ask yourself why all this communication is necessary. When the business was just one entrepreneur, no communication was needed. As the business grew, though, new people joined on, and the business process was split into departments. Many of these splits were done without recognizing the amount of extra communication that would result.

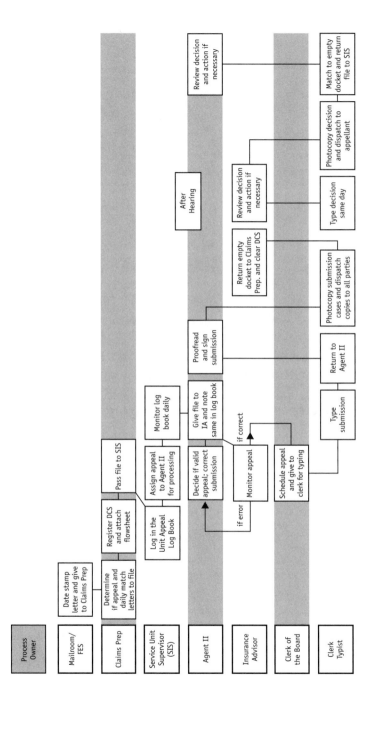

Figure 10-2. An Internal Process Map (Employment Canada)

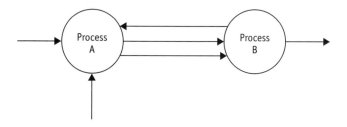

Figure 10-3. A Process Map Showing Back and Forth Communication

As you look at your process map and see large amounts of back and forth communication between two process owners (as in Figure 10-3), you must ask: Is this an area where one person could own both processes? Should we teach Person A the skills of Person B, and develop a self-contained process with one owner?

A good example of this is where managers have developed the keyboard skills of a typist, and the typist has become an administration manager, bringing under control the information retrieval systems in the office. The excessive communication between manager and typist has been eliminated, while at the same time, office information systems have been strengthened.

Process mapping is the tool you use to establish process ownership and take you through these stages:

1. Establishing process ownership

2. Identifying internal customers and suppliers

3. Agreeing on customer requirements

4. Focusing on requirements where nonconformance occurs

Nonconformance means that we are failing to conform to the requirements of our customer. Focusing on nonconformance requires us to use the tool of measurement, discussed in Chapter 11.

BROWSER'S BRIEFING

- Process ownership ensures all people in the organization understand which processes are their responsibility, and who their customers and suppliers are. This was the most overlooked part of quality in the 1980s.
- A strong vision of the future keeps you going during this tough foundation work.
- Mapping the business is followed by mapping the department, then mapping individual processes.
- The unowned processes need to be assigned owners; then people can start agreeing on requirements.
- Identify stages in the process flow where excessive communication occurs.
- Identify "backtracking."
- Eliminate processes that do not add value.
- Reduce cycle time.
- Using measurement, focus on process output requirements that are not being met.

11 | Measurement

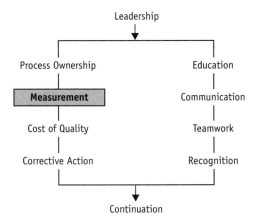

Leadership

Process Ownership   Education

Measurement   Communication

Cost of Quality   Teamwork

Corrective Action   Recognition

Continuation

About six years ago, I was attending a seminar conducted by a good friend of mine, Bart DiLiddo. Bart was previously the CEO of B.F. Goodrich, the tire manufacturer, and was addressing a group of chief executives. In the Q & A session at the end, one CEO asked Bart to define the most important factor that made B.F. Goodrich successful in implementing quality. Bart's answer was unequivocal: "Meaningful measurement."

Two common failings in measurement are:

1. People try to measure something that is unimportant or that they can't influence.

2. The leaders in the organization don't participate in measurement.

That's why going through the process ownership groundwork is so critical. This makes team leaders take ownership of the processes that they want to improve.

MEASUREMENT STEPS

There are five steps, or stages, to measurement:

1. Identify incidents of nonconformance.

2. Record incidents of nonconformance (on a check sheet).

3. Chart incidents of nonconformance (on a graph).

4. Analyze the information that is charted or recorded (to find the cause of nonconformance).

5. Take action to eliminate the cause of nonconformance.

The charting step (3) is not always necessary, but all the other steps are. And yet most people think they are doing "measurement" when they are merely doing that one stage of charting.

Another misunderstanding about measurement is the belief that it is only important when it is "complex" or "scientific." I cannot stress enough the importance of that KISS principle: *Keep it supremely simple,* as the British say.

The way to keep it simple is by placing Step 1, the counting of incidents, and Step 2, the recording of incidents, at the front of your mind, without devoting any time to them. The recording step should not require any calculations as you collect date, but it should constantly focus your mind on what caused this nonconformance, and then cause you to want to change your work process and your behavior pattern.

CHANGING BEHAVIOR

You are probably using measurement all the time in your private life as a way of controlling your family budget, and yet you "haven't got the time" in your working life. Or else, someone does it for you.

Have you ever had a shock phone bill? You analyze which long distance calls are the problem, and change the time when you make a call. You start recording your calls as you make them, and if you have ever done this, you'll agree how amazingly quickly you bring your phone bill under control. As you write down (or record) each incident (phone call), it causes a small change in your behavior. You cut out the mindless chitchat; you stop the peak time phone calls.

Keep it *supremely* simple (KISS) and ensure that measurement does not consume your productive work time. The benefit of measurement is that recording nonconformance makes you *think* about what causes the problem in your process, and you'll be amazed at how you come up with ways of eliminating that problem.

Have you ever tried dieting? A couple of years ago I had to go on a low-fat diet. Every three months I would go back to the doctor and sometimes I'd have done OK, and other times my blood count showed no improvement. The measurement was really too far down the process chain to effect any improvement. I needed to measure at the source of the problem.

One weekend my wife asked me if I'd tried writing down what I ate for each meal. It sounded like a good idea so I drew up a chart. I started Monday morning: for breakfast I wrote in orange juice and cereal, and for lunch I had chicken salad. The evening meal was grilled fish, and I was soon through to Tuesday morning writing in my orange juice and cereal again. Sounds really exciting, doesn't it! By Tuesday lunchtime I was getting a little bored as I wrote in another chicken salad but I stuck to my guns as I ate grilled fish for my evening meal and duly wrote it in on my chart.

Tuesday was a beautiful summer evening and we went for a stroll in the town. We were passing an ice cream stall and without thinking I stopped and bought my favorite butter pecan with chocolate sauce. As we got back home and we walked into the kitchen I saw my diet record and stopped short. I suddenly realized what ice cream with chocolate sauce was going to look like on my low-fat diet record. That entry stared at me all week and made me think far more carefully about what I ate during the rest of the week.

Recording our actions is one of the most powerful ways of changing our behavior. This is what measurement really is.

Measurement has to be conducted by the process owner (who owns the problem). The three stages you go through are collection, tabulation, and display. You'll be surprised at how initially you start measuring the consequences of your problem and then later switch to measuring the causes.

CREATING MEASUREMENT PARTNERSHIPS

The most common mistake I find is that people try to measure something they can't personally influence. Cadet Uniform Services found this problem in the early stages of measurement. They did an outstanding job in laying the foundations of quality, but found it difficult to initiate measurement. A good example of the problem was at the receiving bay. Uniforms were delivered from the customer for cleaning. The customer service driver would drop the uniforms at the bay, and frequently information from the customer was missing. This caused great problems in the processing of uniforms.

The staff on the loading bay started measuring how frequently information was missing, and soon became frustrated. The problems continued the same as ever.

The people who suffer from a problem are often best placed to collect measurement data, but only the people who "own the process" where the problem initiates are in a position to correct the problem.

Cadet saw this and formed partnerships of *internal* customers and suppliers. The receiving bay would keep a check sheet recording incidents when information was omitted, and they would pass this record to the customer service driver, who charted these incidents, and started to identify the causes of the problem and apply corrections.

USING MEASUREMENT TOOLS

A measurement check sheet is the most basic measurement tool, but it can have many different formats. What matters is that you keep it close by you and that you use it.

After tallying on a check sheet, the next step is information display, or graphing. This makes the information pictorial so you can see trends. The method I favor is the bar chart, which combines the check sheet and the graph (see Figure 11-1). You keep this inside a wipe-clean cover and just transfer the data collected on the right over to the left at the end of each month. This is something you should have on display as you use it!

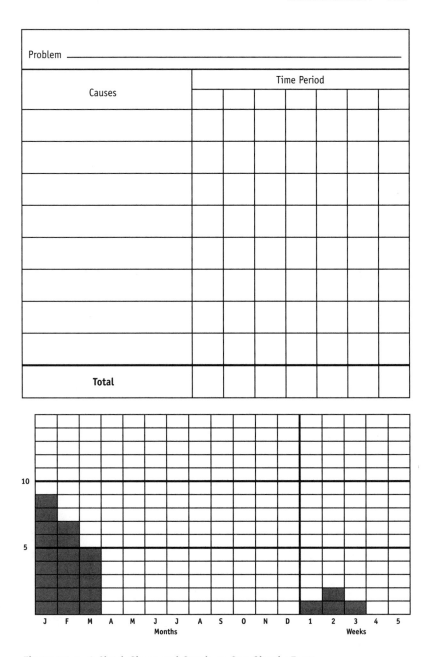

Figure 11-1. A Check Sheet and Graph on One Simple Form

TEAMWORK IN MEASUREMENT

One of the most outstanding examples of the power of measurement I have encountered came from a small town in the Canadian prairies.

About three years ago, Brian Eamer, the manager of a meat processing plant in Moose Jaw, Saskatchewan, attended one of my seminars. The plant he ran was far from a high-tech environment, and it had been experiencing severe delays. He left the seminar keen to find out if measurement really worked. I happened to meet Brian again about three months later, and I only wish I could give you a fraction of his excitement as he told me what had happened.

He had discussed the plant problem with the operators, and they had identified four main causes. To identify the most frequent problem, they started data collection on a simple checkboard at the side of the line.

Each time the line had to be stopped, one of the operators would simply mark down how many minutes were lost in the appropriate column for that type of stoppage. They soon discovered the biggest cause of line stoppages was incorrectly trimmed animal carcasses. Brian was going to talk to his supplier, but first he calculated the true cost of waste of the stoppages. (We'll talk about this in Chapter 12.) He explained the calculation to his supplier, who immediately understood the tens of thousands of dollars' worth of waste. The supplier took quick action, and stoppages were reduced by over 80 percent.

Success didn't stop there. The plant operators, seeing the improvement on the line, focused on other areas of improvement, including general housekeeping. Within a short period, there was a major leap in the plant's profitability. There was also a major improvement in the morale of all staff, as they saw their ability to influence results!

Too often, measurement is thought to be the province of the technical or financial people. The key to success is to lead from the top of your company, and "keep it simple." Brian Eamer was able to communicate the effect of nonconformance to his supplier in a language the supplier understood.

The key points in data collection are:

- Keep it supremely simple (KISS)
- Must not be time-consuming
- Should make you think about the process
- Should make you think about prevention

Team measurement is often a good way of educating people in how to do measurement, or getting people past the initial fear of measurement. The fear aspect arises frequently in the early stages, because people fear that measurement data will be checked by their boss and used to criticize their performance.

USING STATISTICAL PROCESS CONTROL

Statistical process control (SPC) is the tool that has caused more fear and agony than just about any other in the field of quality.

SPC charts and the techniques of SPC are usually imposed on an organization far too soon. You should establish a mood of measurement, total participation in simple measurement, and achieve results from your simple measurement before moving on to SPC. People should graduate to SPC after achieving results using the methods on the previous pages.

SPC, design of experiments, and failure mode and effects analyses are all very worthy tools of quality, but when introduced too early they just reinforce that old message that quality is the province of the quality or technical department.

We all use SPC even though we're not conscious of it, and an example of where you've used it in the past is on your journey to work.

When you first started working at your present location, you probably timed your commute for the first couple of weeks, and got a sense of the typical travel time. You might have found the trip took a half hour, but this varied by plus or minus five minutes, depending on traffic conditions. You worked out that if you left home before 7:55, you would normally arrive at work between 8:20 and 8:30, and so always achieve your start time of 8:30. If you plotted this pattern on a control chart it would look something like Figure 11-2.

In SPC terms, your upper control limit (UCL, the earliest time you arrive) is 8:20, and the lower control limit (LCL, the latest time you arrive) is 8:30. The variation of plus or minus 5 minutes is the natural variation of the process.

As you plot the points on the graph, suddenly one appears below the lower control limit. It's the first week in January, and you arrive at 8:45. Why did this happen? You guessed … a snowstorm, or in SPC terms, "a special cause." In SPC, you learn from special causes, and in real life, you learn from the snowstorm which is a special cause. You check out the weather forecast through January and February, so that you can leave for work in sufficient time to beat the effects of the storm.

AVOIDING FAILURE

So if we go back to the biggest causes of measurement failure, which I described at the beginning of this chapter, it is clear that you need to establish process ownership. The person who owns the process that creates nonconformance must be the person who records the measurement data on the problem. If you own a process that creates nonconformance, whether the process is a meeting, the annual budget, invoicing, or machining a component, you have a responsibility to the rest of the people in your organization to eliminate that nonconformance, whether you are a president, an operator, a salesman, or a supervisor.

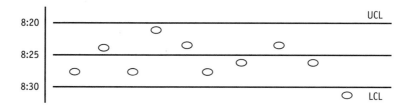

Figure 11-2. An SPC Chart

You may need your customer to feed back measurement data to you, but it is critical that you record the data. Only when you record the data do you start to analyze the data, and only then do you find the root cause of the problem.

Meaningful measurement is the cutting edge of change, and when you have measurement established, you're ready to move on to the most powerful and most misunderstood tool of quality: cost of quality.

BROWSER'S BRIEFING

- Meaningful measurement is the cutting edge of quality improvement.
- Don't measure trivia, and don't measure items you can't influence.
- Visible involvement of leadership in measurement is critical.
- Measurement is simply the recording of events to find out more about a process.
- Recording our actions is also the most powerful way of changing our behavior.
- Build linkages with internal customers and suppliers, and measure together.
- Keep measurement simple, and not time-consuming.
- Use tools such as bar charts or check sheets.
- Use team measurement if individuals are nervous.
- Don't use statistical process control (SPC) until you have developed a measurement culture.

12 | Cost of Quality

You have probably encountered the concept of *cost of quality*. You probably know that few people manage to use it effectively. A few years ago, I met with a U.K. company, Mitel, who used cost of quality very effectively to drive their corrective action system. The methods they used were very simple. Other companies I have worked with in Europe and North America have also been successful through these simple methods.

However, far more companies have not used cost of quality effectively, even though they have been fascinated by this very powerful tool of quality.

WHY THE GREAT INTEREST
IN COST OF QUALITY?

The discovery that 25 percent to 35 percent of your organization's costs are being wasted is a great attention-getter, as Figure 12-1 shows. This waste happens because people are not able to do their job right the first time.

When you express this waste in cold, hard cash, it really focuses your attention on the opportunities for improvement. However, it doesn't stop there; you can now prioritize which problems to work on by feeding the cost of quality (or cost of waste, to be more specific) into your corrective action system. Finally, you can measure your success in improvement through continuous collection of cost of waste, using this data to show the value of your corrective action activity.

So cost of quality does these things:

• Focuses on opportunities for improvement

• Prioritizes opportunities for improvement

• Measures success in improvement

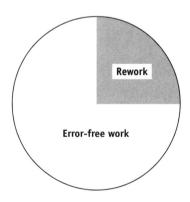

Figure 12-1. The Cost of Waste

Understanding the Concept of Cost of Waste

How did the successful companies make cost of quality work for them?

The first key to success is that everyone in the company should understand the concept of cost of waste. This is the key component of cost of quality.

Look at the process diagram in Figure 12-2. Think of one of the everyday jobs we all do: writing a report for our boss. We all unconsciously use cost of waste to improve the way we write this report.

The process (1) is writing a report, and when we've completed the report, we check it (2) to be sure it meets our boss's requirements. We do this because if our customer (3), the boss, finds any errors, the cost of waste could be much higher!

We spend, say, 20 minutes checking, and find (to our horror) that the numbers don't balance! So we then spend the whole afternoon recalculating and rewriting the report (4).

We learn from this experience.

We're not going to waste four hours of our time (cost of waste) next time we write a report, so we become preventive (5) by writing a checklist (or procedure) and improving our computer skills (training). We also talk to our suppliers who provided the information for the report, and ask them to provide it in a more mistake-proof form next time (6). These may be people who work for us, and we also make sure they understand our requirements. This will help us to avoid having to send

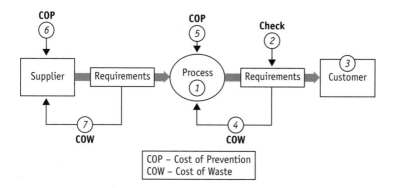

Figure 12-2. A Process Diagram for Corrective Action

incorrect information back to them (7) the next time we have to write a report. These last three actions are cost of prevention items aimed at reducing our own cost of waste.

Whenever information or materials have to be reworked, this is a cost of waste. The four hours we wasted rewriting the report can translate into anything between $250 and $1,250, depending on whether we are an accountant or president of the company. However, take a moment to think of what might have happened had we not checked the report, if it had gone forward and key business decisions had been based on it! The domino effect can be staggering. When you look deep into an organization, you find between one-quarter and one-third of people's time is wasted reworking information or materials. Some people can spend *100 percent of their time* correcting errors. For every $10 million in operating costs, your company is wasting between $2 million and $4 million. Think of the difference if you took half or even a quarter of this to the bottom line. Cost of waste is the driving force behind continuous process improvement.

Integrating Cost of Waste and Continuous Improvement

The second key to success is understanding where cost of waste fits in with the continuous process improvement cycle.

The steps in continuous process improvement are:

1. Identify processes to be improved *(first cut cost of waste)*.

2. Define ownership of processes.

3. Identify customers and suppliers.

4. Agree on requirements.

5. Measure problems.

6. Collect cost of waste *(continuous collection cost of waste)*.

7. Select problems to address *(prioritize using cost of waste)*.

8. Implement corrective action.

9. Continuous improvement *(go back to Step 1)*.

You use cost of waste information in the continuous process improvement cycle in Steps 1, 6, and 7.

At the outset, you use cost of waste to identify which processes are the main cause of your wasted time and materials. You do this by conducting a "first cut" cost of waste calculation. Don't try to find this cost number in your financial records; you'll probably find between 2 percent and 3 percent of your operating costs (a little more if you use activity-based costing). This first cut is a one- or two-day task, which touches each of your managers and supervisors at some point in that time, and will unearth between one-third and one-half of your total cost of waste.

I open a first cut day by briefing the key managers in a business on the principles of cost of quality. This takes about an hour. I then disperse the managers back to their own departments with four key questions, which they will brainstorm with their staff.

1. "Where do you waste time?"

2. "Where do you not know requirements?"

3. "Where do you get problems dumped on you?"

4. "What are your biggest hassles?"

The questions are designed to enable the manager and staff to identify the major time-wasters and hassles in the department, and this also takes about an hour. While they're doing this, I spend time with the CFO, going through the accounts to identify items in the ledger that are cost of waste.

After the brainstorming, the departments then start to quantify and prioritize the items they have listed. By this time, the CFO and I are ready to start visiting with each of the groups and helping to remove any roadblocks, and also feeding any extra items we may have found in the accounts.

That takes us through till lunchtime, and after lunch, we start to feed the groups the cost data they now need. By mid-afternoon, a smaller company would be ready to start consolidation of each department's findings; in a larger organization, this would run into the following day. The end result is a number owned by the people who calculated it, and a great desire to get started in quality improvement.

You will discover after the first cut that most of the processes where problems occur do not have clear ownership. In other words, the boundaries of each process in the business need to be clearly defined, and a person made responsible for the activity inside each set of boundaries.

Steps 2, 3, and 4 in the continuous process improvement cycle involve determining process owners, identifying the internal customers and suppliers for these processes, and getting requirements agreed on. This will take several weeks or even months, depending on the organization.

For this to succeed, you have to create an environment of mutual trust and respect in the organization. This emphasizes the need to work on the *people* skills in parallel with the *process* skills in the change process.

When you have established Steps 2, 3, and 4 in the continuous process improvement cycle, people are ready to start measuring nonconformances on the processes they are responsible for. This is the second point (Step 6) at which cost of waste is used.

Measurement was discussed in Chapter 11, and we saw in that chapter that it doesn't have to be fancy or high-tech to achieve stunning results. Combined with cost of waste, it becomes extremely powerful. Remember how Brian Eamer in Moose Jaw, Saskatchewan, used cost of waste to get his supplier's attention?

Finally, if each process owner can feed their measurement information into a continuous collection system for cost of waste, the whole company will be able to make sound financial choices on which interdepartmental problems should be tackled first. This is the next point (Step 7) in the continuous process improvement cycle where cost of waste is used.

Knowing How to Use Cost of Waste

Having identified the second key to success as knowing where cost of waste fits in the continuous improvement cycle, *the third key to success is knowing how to operate the key points where cost of waste fits.*

I mentioned before that the first cut cost of waste of a one- or two-day exercise which focuses your attention on where your opportunities for improvement exist. You will find about one-third to one-half of your total cost of waste, or to put it another way, you will uncover about $1 million of wasted time and materials for every $10 million of operating costs.

The first cut is the first key point at which cost of waste is used, and it is vital that you calculate this number yourselves, in order to truly believe the opportunities that lie ahead. However, you should have someone who truly understands cost of quality to facilitate the activity, or you won't open all your options, and more importantly in my experience, you'll never get to "end of job."

The second point where cost of waste is used is in conjunction with measurement and data collection.

Again, remember Brian Eamer's meat processing plant in Chapter 11, where he used cost of waste to communicate to his supplier. Those key aspects of data collection were critical to success!

The third point where cost of waste is used is where most people fail to make it happen. This will only work when you have measurement working smoothly, and people really *want* to participate in the improvement process.

I remember Mitel's managing director, David Rayfield, showing me around their facility, and sharing charts like the one shown in Figure 12-3. This chart is typical of what a sales office, for example, might collect as its main problems. Notice that they are only collecting five or six items, so everyone keeps focused on these key issues.

Imagine you are a sales clerk, it is Monday morning, the phone rings, and one of your customers has been short shipped. You deal with the problem, and then you put an entry on the tabulation chart, which is a large white board on the wall of the sales office. Your colleagues see you do this, and it shows your participation in the quality process. Teamwork in action.

Don't give everyone a sheet to fill or they'll forget until the end of the month. Instead, at the end of the week one of the team collects the information on a clipboard. Sharing this with a different person each week makes it teamwork again. Roving supervisors would use three-by-five-inch cards.

Problem Check Sheet					
	Monday	Tuesday	Wednesday	Thursday	Friday
Complaint call	||	|||			
Retyping invoices		|	|		
Rewriting orders	||||				
Credit notes		|	|		
Computer down					

Figure 12-3. A Simple Check Sheet for Problem Measurement

Each week, the check sheets are sent to management information systems (MIS), which is then able to send a monthly cost of waste report back to the department. The calculation data in the MIS software will have been provided by the department when the system was originally set up.

The keys to success in a continuous collection system are:

• Making sure that measurement is working beforehand

• Collecting the data, as opposed to reporting it

• Collecting only five or six items per department

• Using the data to drive the corrective action system

In Mitel, the department teams would review the cost of waste report each month to make decisions on corrective action, and also to check their progress in eliminating problems. They drove down their cost of waste from the typical 25 percent of sales to less than 15 percent in less than two years.

CAN I DO THIS TOO?
WHAT WILL I GET OUT OF IT?

Of course you can make cost of waste work for you, but you do need to follow a well-planned and systematic approach led from the top of an organization. Remember the steps in continuous process improvement, listed on page 138. What you get out of using cost of waste in this framework may surprise you.

I remember asking David Rayfield what had been the biggest effect of quality improvement at Mitel. I expected him to talk about the major turnaround in the profitability of the company. Not so; David said, "I get to go home at six o'clock every night instead of seven o'clock. I spend time with my family which is 'quality time,' and I come to work the next day fresh and ready to go." David had followed those nine steps of continuous improvement.

The first step is a very simple one. A first cut on your cost of quality will get you started. You must get some qualified support, but don't take any shortcuts! And don't lose sight of the purpose of cost of quality, which is to drive corrective action, the subject of the next chapter.

BROWSER'S BRIEFING

- A cost of quality system must be built on the foundation of a measurement system.
- Cost of quality translates measurement data into the common language of business (dollars).
- 25 percent to 35 percent of your organization's costs are wasted because people can't do the job right the first time.
- Seeing the cold hard cash of waste focuses people's attention.
- You can prioritize which problems waste the most money.
- You can measure your success in saving money as corrective action takes effect.
- A "first cut" cost of quality at the outset of your quality journey helps focus on opportunities for improvement.
- Continuous cost of quality collection must occur after measurement is in place.

13 | Corrective Action

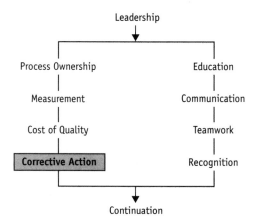

Leadership

Process Ownership   Education

Measurement   Communication

Cost of Quality   Teamwork

Corrective Action   Recognition

Continuation

I remember, in 1985, as chairman of my company's quality management team, initiating a group of "action teams," which were sent out into the business to identify all the areas where "corrective action" was required. I also remember the huge list of problems that these teams dumped on my desk, with no hope of finding solutions. Our building in Wigan, Lancashire, was made famous in George Orwell's novel *The Road to Wigan Pier*. It was over 100 years old, and like every business, we were struggling for cash to finance improvement. People asked for a new elevator system, which would have cost more than a year's earnings. A new air conditioning system would have soaked up more that two years' earnings. Within six months, our quality improvement program was totally discredited through lack of action. We had no system for addressing problems, and no way of choosing which was the most important problem to work on.

Corrective action (C/A) is the bottom line of the quality improvement process. It happens all the way through process ownership, measurement, and cost of quality.

WHAT IS CORRECTIVE ACTION?

The nature of corrective action varies widely. In its simplest form, it may just be two people agreeing to a missing requirement in their day-to-day transactions. At its most complex, it may be a multidisciplinary team involving people from inside and outside the organization working on a problem that affects a wide range of processes. Either way, corrective action means removing the root cause of a problem, and not just applying the quick fixes with which the "fast guns" of the Fortune 500 have made their names over the last 30 years.

In the ultimate "quality world," corrective action would not be necessary. All our processes would be designed in a preventive manner, and there would be no need to correct problems later.

"But," you say, "the real world isn't like that!" We don't always have time for prevention. However, I'm sure you expected the people who designed the local nuclear power plant, or for that matter the people who designed the elevator you used today, to be preventive in their work. When you use cost of quality, you'll find that the cost of prevention is far less than the cost of waste.

One reason your business is wasting money today is because you were not preventive in designing the original process, or you made process changes without building prevention into the new process design.

With this reality in front of you, you've got to use corrective action to design the prevention back into the process. The good news is that the return on investment for this corrective action is still one of the best you'll ever make.

Obstacles

The main obstacle, as you may have guessed, is you. Remember the quote in Chapter 9 about the best firefighters being the arsonists? You have been lighting fires over all these years to show your great fire fighting skills. You want the wonderful return on investment that corrective action will give you, but you're not prepared to make the investment that's needed.

The investment is not cash; you'd do that easily. The investment is time. Leading Japanese companies invest 15 percent of their time in process improvement. If you give only half this time to it, your people will be working four hours a week on corrective action.

That time may simply be spent agreeing on those requirements with their internal customers and suppliers, or it *may* be spent on that corrective action team I talked about. The challenge is to budget time for corrective action, and this will probably be the greatest test of your commitment to quality. This time has to be built into the business plan, and signed off on by key players in your organization. Every person who has someone reporting to them needs to be aware of this time commitment, and to agree to it.

Solutions

Some basic training in the principles of time management will probably be a good investment for you. How else will you manage your time budgets?

Let's revisit the steps in continuous process improvement:

1. Identify processes to improve.

2. Define ownership of processes.

3. Identify customers and suppliers.

4. Agree on requirements.

5. Measure nonconformance.

6. Collect data and calculate cost of quality.

7. Select problems for action.

8. Take corrective action.

9. Continuous improvement.

The first four steps I've talked about in Chapter 10. They are the basics of corrective action: *agreeing on requirements.* These activities should use most of your time in the first three to four months of the improvement process.

The next step, measurement, is where a bit more thinking is required. You start doing measurement to "make you think" (see Chapter 11), and if you don't "think" about what you're measuring, you're wasting your time measuring. To make you think, there is a wonderful and simple corrective action tool called *goal setting.*

GOAL SETTING

Picture yourself as a delivery driver who makes 100 deliveries a week. You're late for 50 deliveries a week, on average—a clear case for corrective action. (If you don't drive a truck, think of the appointments you're late for, or all the other things you could measure to improve.) You won't get down to zero late deliveries in one week. You need to identify the reasons for being late. You need to then set a series of goals for eliminating these root causes. (Figure 13-1 shows a goal made visual as a dashed line on a performance graph.) Perhaps it's rewriting your journey plan, or maybe it's just getting to work on time, or getting on-time maintenance done on the truck. By setting a reduction goal matched against the corrective action you will take, you force yourself to make a change in your behavior, or your process. The time element cuts out the "tomorrow will do" attitude.

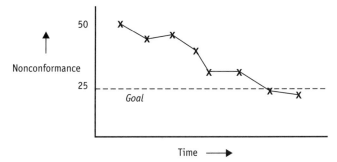

Figure 13-1. A Performance Graph with a Goal Line

PROBLEM SOLVING

Problem solving is what most people think corrective action is all about. I've seen so many fuzzy, touchy-feely approaches to problem solving. You do need an empowered environment to *enable* people to tackle problems freely, but this does nothing for the direct solution of problems. Problem solving is a hard, crunchy business.

Problem solving means first process ownership, and then problem ownership. This is a beginning. People then need an easy-to-remember method which has five, or at most six, steps. The steps must cover these points:

1. Identify the problem.

2. Fix it temporarily.

3. Collect the data.

4. Analyze the cause.

5. Select the solution.

6. Implement and track.

You must have a problem-solving methodology that everyone follows, so the organization talks the same language. A corrective action system is the framework within which this problem-solving methodology is used.

Many companies have all of these tools for solving problems, but more often than not, nothing gets better. The biggest failing is that most companies don't have a system for choosing and tackling the problems they solve. Or they may have a "system," but everyone understands it in a different kind of way.

THE SWAT TEAM TRAP

A lot of organizations get confused by their desire to implement empowerment. They have so much guilt at not having "empowered" in the past that they try to give everyone the power to solve problems immediately. They set up SWAT teams that roam around the company, looking for troubles to shoot. Think about it; you need to know who the enemy is before you start firing guns. SWAT teams simply upset process owners.

If you have a cost of quality system everyone is feeding into, you can tell which are your biggest problems (see Chapter 12). You need a system that enables clear decisions on which problems your scarce resources should tackle, not an anarchic free-for-all.

THE CORRECTIVE ACTION SYSTEM

Most people are surprised when they are told they already have a corrective action system. That's the good news. The bad news is that most corrective action systems are too loose and informal to be effective.

If you are hit with a problem that keeps recurring, you have some choices on how to handle it. You can:

- Solve it.

- Discuss it with a colleague.

- Give it to an expert.

- Ignore it.

Or when you can't get the resources to solve it, then try to persuade your boss to put some muscle behind the effort.

Your boss has similar choices, but perhaps with a bit more influence. You discuss the problem, and when the two of you are unable to resolve it, your boss decides to escalate the matter; this is where the problem starts to lose some of its urgency.

A typical scenario has your boss taking the problem to his or her monthly meeting, in the hope of persuading colleagues to buy in to the need for a solution. This decision is often based more on emotion than on fact, and the organization gradually builds a closet full of skeletons representing the unsolved process problems in the organization. The biggest obstacle is usually that problems are cross-functional, and process ownership is not properly defined.

All too often, a team is established to solve problems, but just fades away in time. You need a crisp and well-defined system for identifying these problems, and then seeing the system through to its conclusion.

The corrective action system should be launched companywide only after establishing process ownership, measurement, and a cost of quality system.

Process ownership means that you get your processes defined, and can identify the skills and membership required for cross-functional corrective action teams.

Measurement means you have "management by fact," and can obtain information for solving problems.

Cost of quality means you can select your problems on a return-on-investment basis, in the way you would approach any other business project.

As you follow each of these steps, you will be resolving problems on a departmental or functional basis, and this provides the foundation for the later work on cross-functional problems.

Your corrective action system should operate in the way you normally approach the resolution of all business problems, but with the difference that you have the discipline of a system that everyone knows and understands.

Any person who identifies a problem should quantify it using measurement data and a cost of quality calculation. If the problem is a routine weekly occurrence, it should also be feeding into the cost of quality system. The cost of quality system should collate problems of a similar nature and feed them into the corrective action system. For example, if a faulty component is causing a problem in a hundred different locations, your cost of quality system will highlight the problem companywide. If a faulty software system is wasting four hours a week at a hundred terminals, the cost of quality system rings alarm bells. Individuals should also be able to blow the whistle on these problems, and they do this through the corrective action system. One-time events are also identified through the corrective action system, and a critical step is for the individual to discuss the problem with his or her boss and agree on the completion of the corrective action form.

This avoids flooding the system with C/A requests, but the presence of a cost of quality system also prevents personality conflicts from stopping the submission of corrective action requests.

The Corrective Action Administrator

A corrective action request form such as the one shown in Figure 13-2 is submitted to the corrective action administrator. The administrator's

Corrective Action Request	
Location:	Date:
Requester:	Phone:
Supervisor:	Phone:
Describe the problem:	
What is the process?	
What is the nonconformance?	
How often does it happen?	
How much waste does it cost each time?	
Time:	
Equipment:	
Material:	
Estimated cost of waste:	
Who can help with this problem?	
What measurements have been taken? Include charts.	

Figure 13-2. A Sample Form for Requesting Corrective Action

job is pivotal. First, he or she maintains a progress log for the management team, which ensures that problems don't get lost; Figure 13-3 shows an example. Once in the log, a problem will be seen through to a conclusion.

Secondly, the administrator assesses the return on investment for tackling a problem, and this determines whether a problem will progress to formation of a C/A team (or a "process improvement team," if you prefer).

Thirdly, the administrator has to identify the senior process owner, or sponsor, for the C/A problem, and make sure the sponsor establishes a well-designed team to tackle the problem.

Finally, the administrator feeds back process information to the management group and ensures that resources are directed where the company requires them.

Corrective Action Administrator Log

Today's Date _____5/16/96_____   Page _____5_____

Log Number	35	36	37	
Date Received	4/5	5/1	5/15	
Originator	S. Mastroianni	M. Finch-Grover	G. McEnroe	
Problem Definition	prices omitted from invoices	machine breakdown	stock of incorrect raw materials	
C/A Assignee or Evaluation	F. Alomar	D. Ellington	S. Mastroianni	
Last Status Report	4/25/91	5/15/91		
Status Due	2 weekly	2 weekly	4 weekly	
Which Step	3	2	1	
What Action Is Planned	Measurement Check Sheet			
Date Closed				

Figure 13-3. A Sample Corrective Action Administrator Log

A corrective action team is really a process improvement team. The people involved in the process should be on the team, and special skills, such as finance and data processing, are drafted into the team as needed. The team works through the problem, using the problem-solving methodology which you have in-house, and which will be similar to that described earlier in the chapter.

Team membership may fluctuate, and you may be down to as few as two people when doing the final measurements on the effectiveness of your solution. When the problem is solved, the team disbands.

Nothing remarkable, you may say. But corrective action is more a case of discipline and perseverance, a bit like good police work.

We've progressed through the four stages of process improvement, and it is essential while you address them that you work in parallel on the development of the culture in your organization. This is the subject of the four chapters in Part V.

BROWSER'S BRIEFING

- Corrective action means eliminating problems that cause non-conformance in a process output.
- Corrective action may simply mean two people agreeing on requirements.
- Corrective action may involve a multidisciplinary team working on a complete business problem.
- Corrective action means avoiding "quick fixes."
- Ultimately, processes should be designed preventively to avoid the need for corrective action.
- The stages in continuous process improvement are:
  1. Identify processes to improve.
  2. Define ownership of processes.
  3. Identify customers and suppliers.
  4. Agree on requirements.
  5. Measure nonconformance.
  6. Collect data and calculate cost of quality.
  7. Select problems for action.
  8. Take corrective action.
  9. Continuous improvement.
- Improvement can be driven by a simple tool, like goal setting.
- Your organization should have a standard problem-solving methodology:
  1. Identify the problem.
  2. Fix it temporarily.
  3. Collect the data.
  4. Analyze the causes.
  5. Select the solution.
  6. Implement and track.
- Avoid SWAT teams. Problems should be solved by the people who own the process with skills and knowledge added on an as-needed basis.
- Your organization needs a closed-loop corrective action system.
- Leading Japanese companies invest up to 15 percent of people's time in process improvement activity once they've completed their initial education.

PART V

THE PEOPLE

14 | Education

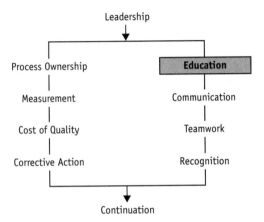

Leadership

Process Ownership   **Education**

Measurement   Communication

Cost of Quality   Teamwork

Corrective Action   Recognition

Continuation

A good friend of mine, Brian Dalzell, was speaking about education at a quality conference I chaired. He related how his daughter had recently returned from school and had mentioned that the class spent the morning on sex education. In this enlightened age, Brian said, he was pleased at the news. He then asked the audience to visualize themselves in the same situation, and asked how they would feel if their own child were instead to return from school with the story that they had received sex *training* that day.

In quality there has been a lot of education but a lot less training. Putting it in everyday terms, companies invest in word processing or spreadsheet software, yet few people fully use the capability of that software. Those organizations that have invested in their people to develop the skills of their software users are getting the real return on investment. Too many times, a budget is expended on hardware and software, and the training is left to take care of itself. Technology will give you an edge for a while, but as it becomes more accessible to the competition, your ability to use that technology is really what sets you apart.

The ability to learn faster than the competition is the only competitive edge your organization possesses. You've probably heard the saying, whatever your business: "There are no secrets in this industry: people who do it better get the business."

In England in the 1950s, there was a legendary robbery led by a villain named Ronald Biggs. It was called the Great Train Robbery. What we are going to talk about here is the Great *Training* Robbery. The millions that have been wasted through badly designed and inappropriate training are becoming a legend in themselves.

The opportunities for waste and error are enormous. You may recall Masaaki Imai's comment that everyone has two jobs: the job they do, and improving the way they do their job. So education and training fall into two categories. First, the education and training you need to do your existing job. Whether it is accounting or metalwork, operating computer software or carrying out machine maintenance, we always have areas of skills and knowledge. However, we also need to *improve:* if you are, say, a senior executive, how are your keyboard skills when you operate that wonderful new laptop computer you just acquired?

ACQUIRING SKILLS AND KNOWLEDGE FOR IMPROVEMENT

So we will focus first on the skills and knowledge you will need to operate your improvement activities.

When you begin quality improvement, you almost certainly discover a skill and knowledge deficiency—but attending a one-day seminar doesn't give the attendee a degree in total quality management. You don't deal with these deficiencies with a crash course in the way cramming helped you pass an exam at school.

Many people who run organizations think of education and training in terms of the paradigm they acquired when they went to school. Education is something given in big chunks. Everyone gets the same, and if you throw enough of it at people, some of it will stick. Training is thought of as verbally repeating the procedures for carrying out a job that is simple for the instructor, and a total mystery for the trainee.

The secret to successful education is "just-in-time" education. You may recall my mentioning an education specialist in Ontario named Treat Hull. His words at an ASQC conference in 1992 still stick in my mind: "The half-life of education is about 30 days." Put another way, you will have totally forgotten half of what you learn within the first month, unless you have put that knowledge into practice. *If you don't use it, you lose it.*

TOP MANAGEMENT'S
QUALITY EDUCATION PROGRAM

All of this underlines the need to plan your quality education very carefully, and to line it up alongside your process improvement activity. This applies right from the top of the organization. Your leadership should be putting into practice their new knowledge every bit as much as the administrative staff and operations people do. There must be specific workplace activities between each piece of education that is acquired.

Quality education must first show the management team how to design and operate new organizational systems, and then show everyone in the organization how to design and operate new job processes. Your organization needs to know how to apply improvement at both the macro and the micro level.

One of the common misunderstandings in education is that once the initial burst is over, then no more time needs to be invested in "improvement." Successful Japanese companies invest up to 15 percent of their time in continuous improvement. This means six to seven hours a week. You should be planning to do something like this on an ongoing basis once your initial education is complete.

The initial education should involve the "team" that leads an organization, and for an organization of up to 300 people, this will be between six and ten people. This group needs to understand all the issues we are discussing in this book, and needs to take ownership of the change process during the initial education period.

You can accomplish this initial education of the leadership team with a three- or four-day "immersion," which is definitely the best way. However, many organizations are unable to pull their senior management out of the business for this long. One day a week following the agenda in Figure 14-1 enables the team to start implementing changes as they move along, and this also avoids information overload. The downside of the one-day-a-week approach is that the conversion, and therefore commitment, to quality is not as strong as in the four-day immersion.

Either way, the team must start doing things in a different way, and demonstrate to the rest of the organization that change is starting to happen. The whole management education should be lighting the fuse for everyone else in the company.

You should also feed the hunger for knowledge this initial education creates. Feed people with books, audiotapes, and the like. Avoid "heavy" books and use cassette tapes as much as possible; a tape played during the daily commute can act almost as "subliminal" learning. Most major books are available on tape these days, and the tapes provide a good overview before reading the book.

Feed the management team with seminars on the aspect of quality which will be their specialty, and create an atmosphere of learning throughout the organization.

The education strategy must flow from the management team out into the organization (you could say "from the top down"). The management team must now develop a plan to deploy education on quality to *every person* in the organization.

I find most companies do a very bad job in planning their education, and an even worse job in communicating the plan to people in the organization. In building the plan, you need to remember things like vacations and periods of high activity in the business cycle. Avoid these totally. Even if people attend your training, their minds will be elsewhere. You generally also need to give people a month's notice, and the commercial and technical people even longer, in order to ensure they will be available.

Quality Management Team: Education, Planning, and Implementation

The leaders of an organization study in detail the principles of quality and establish a quality management team (QMT) and a quality policy. They define their roles as members of the QMT, and also as managers of a business function where they will implement quality. They learn in detail how to manage change in their organization using the change process. The management team plans to evaluate the cost of waste in their organization and build a plan for dealing with the wasted resources of the organization.

------------------------------ Day 1 ------------------------------

Introduction
- Course purpose and structure
- The need for improvement
- Defining quality
- Delivering quality
- Improving quality
- Measuring improvement
- *Video*

- Baldrige criteria
- ISO 9000
- Maturity grid

Leadership
- Managing change
- The change process
- Capacity to change

- *Video*
- Leadership in quality
- Quality policy
- Commitment
- The management team
- Roles and responsibilities
- QMT workshop case study

------------------------------ Day 2 ------------------------------

Process Ownership
- The sequence for continued improvement
- The need for process ownership
- Customer workshop
- *Video*
- Process flow
- Cycle time reduction
- Key tasks workshop
- Establishing requirements

Measurement
- Fear of measurement
- Measurement sequence
- Data collection
- Measurement tabulation
- Action plan
- Measurement check sheet
- Measurement display
- SPC
- Measurement and problem solving
- Measurement case study

Education
- Education and the QMT
- Education plan
- Continuous improvement system
- Work improvement system
- Manager's responsibility
- Problem solving
- Skills workshop

------------------------------ Day 3 ------------------------------

Communication
- Interpersonal communication
- Team briefing
- Publicity
- Publicity workshop
- Networking
- Teamwork questionnaire

Teamwork
- Team needs
- The quality management team

- Meetings
- *Video*
- Teamwork questionnaire
- The team leader

Recognition
- A recognition system methods
- Activities workshop
- Whom to recognize
- How to recognize
- Recognition workshop

Cost of Quality
- Cost of waste
- Cost of prevention
- The waste in an organization worksheet
- How to use cost of waste
- First cut—cost of quality
- Continuous collection workshop

------------------------------ Day 4 ------------------------------

Corrective Action
- Continuous improvement sequence
- Three approaches to corrective action
- Goal setting
- Problem solving
- Root cause analysis

- Selecting solutions
- Problem solving workshop
- Corrective action system
- System procedure
- System flow
- System documents
- Corrective action workshop

Continuation
- The need to plan
- The second "cycle"
- Celebration day
- The new team
- The new challenge
- *Video*
- Planning workshop

Figure 14-1. A QMT Education Agenda

Planning and scheduling is an art as well as a science, and you should use the skills of your production planners or operation schedulers to help the education specialists do the planning.

Most management teams are so "hot to trot" that they want to do something immediately once they've finished their own education, so use the intervening month to work on your new systems, like communication, corrective action, and recognition. Then when the second phase of education arrives, you will have something concrete to show people. Remember, when people learn skills like problem solving and communication, they will need enhanced systems within your organization in order to use these skills.

PROMOTING EDUCATION IN THE REST OF THE ORGANIZATION

The *Oxford Dictionary of Quotations,* under "Education," quotes from Lord Brougham (sixteenth century), who allegedly said, *"Education makes people easy to lead, but difficult to drive."* Education is without question the first step in achieving change in the culture of your organization.

For the rest of the people in the organization to participate in the change process, they now need to acquire the people skills, like communication and teamwork, and the process skills, like measurement and problem solving. Unquestionably, the most powerful way they can acquire these skills is by tutoring from their supervisors. The best way to know your subject is to teach it; this approach requires supervisors to learn and understand the new skills, and develops the work group into a team that can tackle the problems of their own work environment.

The time commitment for this second phase of education should be about two hours a week in the formal education setting, but each individual should be committing another half-hour to an hour a week, either alone or with the work group, tackling work problems in the workplace. An agenda I use for this piece of education is shown in Figure 14-2.

Continuous Improvement Training

All employees require training that is designed to provide them with the knowledge and skills necessary to improve the way they work. Sessions address specific stages in solving a problem. Participants carry out practical exercises, workshops, and assignments on problems they select. The course content is as follows:

Introduction *Why are we here?* gives a background in total quality management, and shows the benefits it offers to employees and the organization itself. This session is conducted immediately before Session 1.

Session 1 *Why work together?* looks at the dynamics of teamwork and what makes a successful team. We discuss the selection of team members and techniques for making team participation more effective and enjoyable.

Session 2 *How do we work?* looks at the importance of customer satisfaction and extends the idea to include internal customers. This leads to process ownership and understanding our customers' expectations.

Session 3 *How well do we work?* introduces the concept of prevention. We begin to analyze our work processes, and to define our expectations of our suppliers.

Session 4 *How can we work better?* presents a six-step process to identify and eliminate problems. In this session we look at the first four steps, in which we identify the problem, define the process, put in place a temporary fix, and identify the root causes of the problem.

Session 5 *What do mistakes cost?* defines the cost of waste and those activities that contribute to it. We learn to calculate this cost and to use the results to gain management support.

Session 6 *How do we eliminate the problem?* returns to the six-step process begun in Session 4. We learn how to determine all the possible solutions to our problem, and to select the most appropriate.

Session 7 *Where do we go from here?* reviews the quality journey that we have made since the start of the sessions, and directs us in planning where we will next use the continuous improvement process in our work.

Figure 14-2. An Agenda for a Quality Training Course for Employees

The critical activity where most failure occurs is in application and follow-up coaching between formal education sessions. Just-in-time education means employees must work with the new tools they've acquired within 48 hours of completing an education session. Remember, if they don't use it, they'll lose it.

CONTINUING EDUCATION

This whole burst of education will cause you to realize how much can be gained from a long-term education strategy. Use this newfound enthusiasm to identify which job skills people need to develop further.

Let's look at education first. Do you know what you already know? A basic inventory of your existing skills and knowledge is a great way to identify the skills, and the level of those skills, for each of the processes in your business. Which are your problem processes, and how will improved skills help?

I usually get a group to brainstorm the question, *"Which skills would I like to improve in order to improve service to my internal and external customers?"* The areas that most organizations have to focus on come as no surprise: time management, computer skills, listening, presentation skills, and assertiveness.

You also need to analyze the skill sets required for each of your work activities. One of the great benefits of an ISO 9000 audit or your work procedures is that you identify the skill requirements for each of the jobs in your business. When you've done this, an assessment of the skills your people have in hand will show the gap. This gap analysis provides you with your training requirements for the short and medium term.

Finally, you need to ask yourself the following questions:

- Is there a training plan for the next two to three years?

- Does my organization have an inventory or registry listing employee skills?

- Is the listing available for management use?

- Is there a method for identifying training needs?

- Do our training methods suit the audience?

- How much time is spent orienting new employees?

You've probably started to ask yourself how much all this will cost. Go back to your cost of quality calculation, and them remind yourself of that T-shirt logo which seems to be everywhere these days:

"If you think education is expensive, try ignorance."

BROWSER'S BRIEFING

- *"The ability to learn faster than your competitors may be the only sustainable advantage."*—Arie de Geus
- Education and training are needed for the job you already do.
- Education and training and needed for improving the job you do.
- The old "school" paradigm of giving education and training in large, uniform chunks is not effective for quality education within business organizations.
- Successful education is given on a "just-in-time" basis.
- Leading Japanese companies invest 15 percent of people's time in process improvement activity once they've completed their initial education.
- The management team must be educated first, and as a team.
- Education and training must then be dispersed through the rest of the organization, and are most effective when related to specific business problems.
- Feed people with books and audiotapes.
- *"Education makes people easy to lead, but difficult to drive."*—Lord Brougham
- Supervisors will become "team coaches" in tomorrow's organization. They should be trained in how to be trainers.
- Analyze your business processes by evaluating the skills required to operate them, the skills you already have, and the gap between the two.
- This gap indicates your future training needs.
- *"If you think education is expensive, try ignorance."*

15 | Communication

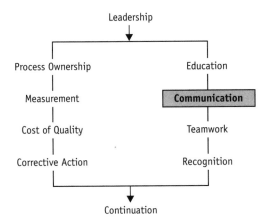

Since 1966, we've added 60,000 words to the English language. Each year one million scientific articles are published in 40,000 different journals around the world. Media growth has dulled our senses, and the motto of many news media has become "if it bleeds, it leads." We are deluged with sensations vying for our attention in a vast sea of information. Unsolicited information, both at home and work, has become our biggest nightmare.

Most of the waste of time your organization experiences is the result of poor communication. In Chapter 8, I described how organizational structure is one of the big barriers to communication. Your span of communication is usually about six people, but few realize that the depth to which even the best communicators can penetrate is only three layers of an organization. Here I mean communication (which includes feedback), and not motivation or manipulation. Recruiting people with good communication skills (not just "interview" skills) and developing the skills of your existing employees is one of the fundamental investments you must make if quality is going to happen. Developing communication systems is the other area you must address. Your organization's communications must be addressed at the interpersonal level in terms of skills, and at the organizational level in terms of systems. Let's look at person-to-person communication first.

INTERPERSONAL COMMUNICATION

One of the best organizations I've come across that specialized in communication is the NLP Institute. NLP stands for neuro-linguistic programming. Over the years, the Institute has used the NLP approach to analyze human behavior. In their analysis, people communicate through three main channels: audio (words), visual (images), and kinesthetic (feelings). Different nations and cultures have different balances of these components. The British communication is mainly audio; they wrap everything in words. U.S. Americans are far more visual. People from Mediterranean nations tend to communicate far more through their feelings. Do you know the balance of communication inside your own company culture? Do you know who is a picture person and who is a word person? Accountants are often audio, designers tend to be visual; perhaps your salespeople communicate with feelings. The key point is that until you work with each other's "channel" for messages, your messages will fly off into infinity, without being received at their intended destination.

Neuro-linguistic programming is a system for working with channels other than your own—sending your message in words, images, or feelings (Laborde 1983). My wife is American and an accountant, so she's more verbal than many Americans. I'm British, but come from a family of artists, and so I'm more visual than many British. Doing an NLP "calibration" exercise helped us in understanding why Britain and the United States are two nations separated by a common language.

If the people inside your organization are going to communicate more effectively, they need to understand their channels of communication. Don't just send everyone to a communication course and think that is all that you need to do. Communication is a practical day-to-day activity that all of us (including you) have to work to improve. Don't assume you are a good communicator. You may be good with words, but what are the messages you send emotionally?

Another area of interpersonal communication you need to understand and also to respect is your "sixth sense." Gut feeling is important, but we have been trained to respect it less and less. Your sixth sense is simply recognizing the messages you receive that do not come strictly through verbal communication. Albert Mehebrian did work in this area, and found that over 80 percent of the messages we send and receive are nonverbal signals and signs. Our body language is far more powerful than we realize. This is work you will need to do on your own or with a counselor, but I can promise you that until you understand your own communication modes, you will not be aware of the difficulty you may be causing around you through miscommunication.

Using Communication Technology

The simplest form of communication was always the handwritten or typed memo, but with the advent of voice mail and electronic mail, it has become even easier to communicate. The difficulty is that we have tended to send more messages over a wider area, instead of focusing on key messages, and ensuring that these are properly understood. I am sure you, like me, suffer from a crippling overload of junk mail, both from internal and external sources. Your process analysis in Chapter 10 tells you the critical people you should communicate with, and we must focus on these targets more accurately. Key communications need to be written *and* oral. The written must be concise (the key points only); the oral support then reduces the paper your receiver must deal with. The blend of fax or e-mail with voice mail does this as well.

It's no surprise that organizations have invested so much in communications technology, but so few have invested in the people skills of how to use this technology. I don't mean the technical skills. I mean the skills we need to prevent information systems from being a way of dumping problems, instead of finding solutions. People must know their key customers, and send messages in a way the customers can handle.

However, this written or oral communication is less than 20 percent of the communication that goes on between people. That's why organizations that put their employees in little shoebox cubicles with computer terminals are experiencing morale and communication problems.

Body Language

Nonverbal communication accounts for most of the messages we send and receive. Body language, as we have come to know it, tells more about us than we care to realize. Our eyes, our lips, our shoulders, our arms are telling people what we feel. Our actions send signals to others. You know that if you tell your children to straighten their rooms, but the rest of the house is a mess, they will follow their visual example. What does your office desk look like at this moment? It's sending a signal to all the people you work with, and it's telling them whether or not you're in control of your work processes. (Contrary to what the popular poster says, a tidy office is not a sign of a sick mind.)

Nonverbal messages have a more powerful force than you may realize. I once heard speaker Joe Mancusi talk on the topic of what makes some people more successful than others. Right up front, he was clear that telling the truth was the biggest factor in success. Recall the research by James Kouzes and Barry Posner cited in Chapter 9: more than anything else, people want leaders who tell the truth. If your verbal messages don't fit with your nonverbal messages, people will get mixed messages. Even if they apparently accept your verbal message, subconsciously they are unable to do so. Their intuition tells them something doesn't jive. The nonverbal messages we send are critical.

Intuition

If you want a book that opens your eyes and stimulates your feelings, then try *The Intuitive Manager* by Roy Rowan. Please understand that I am not for one moment suggesting that you abandon "management by fact." I am telling you that far more "facts" are coming at you than you realize, and the more facts you use, the better you will operate.

Intuition, like so much I've discussed, is material for another entire book. However, I do encourage you to learn to trust your intuition. It is fed by hard facts, as well as the body language you receive from others, and it's simply processed in a high-speed fashion to give you conclusions which may seem surprising. A well-developed intuition receives the nonverbal messages, processes them, and feeds the correct conclusions to your outer mind. Your challenge is to first develop your reception channels, and then trust the output from your intuition process.

The other responsibility your organization has is to provide channels for communication and time to use those channels.

VERTICAL COMMUNICATION

The Industrial Society is a British professional society dedicated to improving business performance. It has done excellent work promoting a vertical structure for communication through the technique of "team briefing." People who have used the technique say it has encouraged involvement and participation throughout their organization. Team briefing is a really simple and formalized version of what you may well do already, but perhaps on a sporadic basis. The chief executive should brief his or her immediate reports (four to eight people) once a month. In 20 minutes, the key points of business activity during the previous month are outlined. Other executives are provided with a written core brief of no more than a page, and they are responsible for briefing their own staff within the next 24 hours. In a three-layer organization, you should have communicated with all your people within 72 hours.

The first key factor in successful team briefing is delivering the information *face to face*. This gives the nonverbal as well as the verbal message. Given time, it also creates a better opportunity for two-way communication. Next, the group size should be between 6 and 12 people. Smaller groups discourage people from speaking, and larger groups don't give people opportunity to speak. The briefing should be given by the team leader. Delegating the job tells the team that the information is not important. If the information is not important, it shouldn't be in the briefing.

Regularity in the briefing builds trust in the team. The frequency should be tied to the financial reporting of the business, and ideally should be monthly. Once that is decided, everyone should block the date and time for the next six meetings. The session itself should last about 30 minutes.

The information, in brief, should be relevant to the team, and to the individuals in that team. Two-thirds of the brief should be "local" information. The remaining third is the "core brief" about the larger organization.

Team briefing leads to better knowledge about important issues, less misunderstanding, more credibility for the team leader, and better linkage of the team to the organization as a whole.

Finally, monitoring the results of the briefing ensures that any shortcomings in the briefing can be eliminated. Local information should always be double-checked before the briefing. Having another member do the briefing with the team leader sitting with the team can lead to improvement ideas. Checking with individuals after the briefing identifies shortcomings.

People are happy to listen when the information is relevant and the session is well run.

As the briefing becomes expected throughout the organization, it develops into a channel where messages will also flow up as well as down. Team briefing cannot be the only tool or technique; it must be used alongside improved interpersonal skills and the other important communication tools.

HORIZONTAL COMMUNICATION

Networking happens already in your organization, but the output from networking sessions is probably not used to benefit the organization. I'm thinking of the lunchroom conversation. We all joke about things overheard at the water cooler, and of course when a group travels or eats dinner together, the exchange of information can be very powerful.

Team briefing improves vertical communication, but remember that communication within our internal customer/supplier chain is horizontal. Networking must contain horizontal communication. Networking is often left to chance. You need to provide regular networking opportunities and take out that random element.

The barrier you are attacking here is often called the "fortress mentality." Departments, in their eagerness to build team spirit, unknowingly build fortress walls against other departments and even compete against other departments who should be their own customers or suppliers.

In addition to the manufacturing facility I used to run, the business had a chain of concession shops in major retail stores. I remember the first time we mixed the retailing and manufacturing supervisors. The results were electric, and the interchange of ideas was phenomenal. The manufacturing people were given new ideas on packaging, and the retail people has their eyes opened to new product possibilities they had never thought about before.

Another type of networking involves bringing together people from different parts of the organization who do similar work but who rarely meet. Your annual sales meeting is a good example of this. Now let your mind run laterally and apply the idea of the "sales meeting" to department supervisors or to operators or clerks from different parts of the organization. Don't just throw them together, though. Provide a framework, an agenda, a structure.

PROVIDING COMMUNICATION TOOLS

Finally, people need good communication tools to use within the system and the environment you've created. Identify the special communication channels that you want to strengthen. Philip Crosby advocated a tool he called the Error Cause Removal memo. To quote his words, *"Workers have great difficulty in communicating to management those things which stop them from doing a job right the first time."* Sadly, too few have understood Crosby's words about this delicate but important communication tool; many people have installed a corrective action tool instead of a method of communication.

Simple-to-use tools for communicating recognition are also important. Chapter 17 on recognition will describe the "Bravogram" created by Bob Latham at Bell Mobility. This method of supporting and encouraging recognition was a powerful communication tool in the company.

Telephones, faxes, and modems are only some of the tools you can use to improve communication. Develop the paper tools such as the Bravogram as well. However, remember to use them within a properly designed communication system where interpersonal, vertical, and horizontal communication have all been developed.

BROWSER'S BRIEFING

- Poor communication is the primary cause of failure to deliver on customer promises.
- Organizations must be designed to enable effective communication.
- Individuals must be recruited with or trained to have good communication skills.
- Individually, we need to be aware of which are our primary channels of communication: audio (words), visual (images), or kinesthetic (feelings).
- Verbal communication accounts for less than 20 percent of the communication between North Americans.
- Simply providing a high tech communications system will not improve communication. People need to learn the "art" of using these systems.
- When people can freely tell the truth, and also have the courage to hear the truth, organizations communicate more effectively.
- Intuition provides individuals with a lot of nonverbal communication, but it is rarely trusted.
- Structured briefing of all persons in an organization enhances the outward flow, and also the feedback, of information.
- Horizontal communication must be fostered along the lines of process flow of the business as the quality organization develops.
- The organization must provide a framework and tools to facilitate communication, whether it is notification of problems or saying "thank you" for solutions.

16 | Teamwork

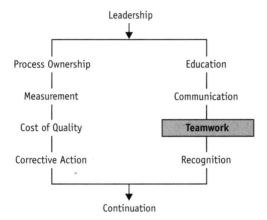

By the age of 30, most sensible people have given up playing vigorous physical sports. But readers who have played a team sport like rugby or basketball will have made some of your lifelong friendships from the game and will still thrill at the poetry and flow of teamwork that you see on the field. I was never a star at rugby, but like so many who engage in a sport or hobby while growing up, I played for the love of the game.

At 30 years old, when many of my peers had switched to weekend gardening, I was still playing rugby, and my club asked me to captain one of the teams. I was both honored and panic-stricken. I had no experience of leadership in either work or sport, and I could only barely get my place on the team through ability. I still visit the Davenport Rugby Club whenever I return to England, and I thank the club for the opportunity they gave me to learn about leadership and teamwork.

Leadership and teamwork are two areas of quality that are inextricably intertwined, and the three years I spent captaining the Davenport Dukes taught me more about leadership than any MBA course ever could. Too often teamwork in the quality context is a theoretical activity. It's either a classroom activity, or a "team-building game."

When I took the job, the Dukes were losing every game and few people wanted to play. I knew from being a team member that more than anything else, the players hated playing "short" (with a player missing). They felt beaten before they started. That first year we didn't win too many games, but we never played short. I knew that the one thing I could give the team was a full playing side, and I worked myself into the ground doing that. A better team would rob us of a key player on a Friday night or even on Saturday morning, but we never gave up, and we never played short. The players recognized this, and by the second year they were prepared to stand down as reserves for the Dukes some weeks because there were so many who wanted to play. By the end of two years, the team had been nicknamed within the club as "Merrill's Marauders."

Ask yourself what you can give your team. When you were a team member before you became a leader, what did you want from the leader? Could it be short, well-run meetings? Concise paperwork? Could it be help in problem solving? Give your skills to your people, and they will come together as a team.

I was good at organizing the Dukes, but I wasn't the side-stepping running-back type the team craved for. I certainly didn't understand forward play. On the field, I gave over the running of the forwards to a bearded mountain of a man called Andy Altree and the running of the backs to an Irish wizard called Brendan Webb. These two stalwarts called the shots in the minute-to-minute tactical moves, and I took orders from them as the game unfolded. They knew their part of the game far better than I did. I played on the wing, which was the perfect position to view the strategy of the game. I stress that I didn't do this out of managerial enlightenment; it was practical necessity. My role was to plan the strategy of the game.

Take time to identify the skill areas that your team members possess and take time to develop the skill areas that are needed. All this takes time, time, and time. If you give this to your people, they will give back your investment many times over. You can't be the leader in every situation, so learn to share the leadership role. Ray Kroc of McDonald's once said, "No one of us is as good as all of us."

One thing that everyone on that Dukes team knew was that if ever anyone dropped a ball, the last thing they needed was a barrage of groans from the rest of the team. We all knew we had let them down. I had once played for a captain who would humiliate his players in front of the rest of the team (and in front of the opponents). We all realized that encouragement and building people's belief in themselves were the way to eliminate bad play. That doesn't mean a team of wimps; it means a team of people who tackle hard, run hard, and fight the opposition and not themselves.

THE TEAM

What are the principles on which your team operates? Do you encourage each other or do you argue regularly? Do you talk honestly and openly with each other or are there hidden agendas? Are your meetings hard, concise, and to the point, or do you wallow around being nice and avoiding the truth?

The foundation for all of the good practices is trust and respect. Trust and respect come slowly and you build it after hours. A big part of the Dukes' team building came in the bar after the game. We learned about each other, became friends, and built trust. You can try complex analyses of everyone in the organization—or you can simply give everyone the opportunity to understand how the rest of the people on their team behave and what makes them tick.

There are two general routes for building a team's trust. One is activity-oriented, and gives a visible sense of achievement. The second is exploratory, and gives people a chance to discover their respective frames of reference in a relaxed environment.

I'm deeply involved in the American Society for Quality Control (ASQC), a misnomer for the world's largest organization devoted to quality improvement in all walks of life, from kindergarten to the boardroom. The membership and leadership of each chapter are entirely voluntary, but everyone draws from the greatest source of quality knowledge that you could ever hope to find.

In the summer of 1993, the executive of the chapter to which I belong conducted a strategic planning session which was led by David Luke, a lecturer from Queen's University in Kingston. David started the session by pointing out that we did not know each other. I suddenly realized how a voluntary organization is so different from a business organization. We met each other once or twice a month, and didn't even know which side of the city we all came from. David paired us off, and asked us to discuss our background with our neighbor, and to say what we most wanted to achieve in life. Our neighbor then had the task of telling our individual story to the rest of the group. The hour we spent doing this built the most remarkable understanding among us all.

We were increasing the overlap in our frame of reference by discovering what we had in common, and building our mutual trust and respect. When you know where someone was born and grew up, where they went to school, and what their activities and goals are in life, that person then takes on a third dimension. They cease to be merely a cardboard cutout. This builds trust and understanding between you.

Riding the Rapids as a Team

I recall my first experience with the activity-oriented approach. In 1985, Courtaulds sent me and a group of 20 executives to a two-week leadership development course at Clemson University in South Carolina. In the middle of the course, we were all taken into the Georgia mountains for an activity weekend.

We'd heard rumors about the Chattooga River's whitewater, and someone mentioned that the movie *Deliverance* had been filmed on the stretch of water we would be experiencing. We stayed Friday night in a log cabin in the woods, and I was sufficiently impressed by the rumors to ensure I had an early night. Unlike some of the group, I decided to avoid late-night drinking at a country-and-western bar.

The next day, we woke at 6 a.m. and drove to a simple southern shack, where we were served a "last breakfast" of ham and eggs over easy, home fries, and grits. You must realize that for simple English boys, these words were totally foreign, and the food even more so. By now, we had discovered that people had actually died on the Chattooga River. What we were unsure of was whether it was the whitewater or the grits that caused their demise. The tension was rising, and no one was prepared to admit they were "chicken."

Feeling like condemned men who'd eaten a hearty last breakfast, we set off for the river, and upon arrival were split into groups and introduced to our guides. I remember my first feeling of security when our group met Rolie, the bearded athletic giant who was to guide us through the perils that lay ahead.

I remember his first instruction being to "wet our feet and feel the river." As we climbed into the river raft which would be our home for the next four hours, we admired the magnificent calm of the river and the wonderful tree-lined shore. We moved slowly with the current, and as we rounded the first bend, we began to hear a small roar. Rolie shouted strict orders: "Brace your knees on the side of the raft, and if you fall, fall inwards!" We were approaching the first of the rapids, and the advice seemed very sensible.

It must have happened in seconds, and yet it seemed to last a lifetime. We traveled at incredible speed between predatory outcrops of granite, which seemed poised to tear us apart and consume us without a trace. But then it was over, and we were again in calm water.

Our group looked at each other. We were intact, and the feeling of exhilaration was indescribable. One person yelled, another screamed. The tension had been released, or had it? We had a sense of achievement, but then we heard another roar, and this was only a few seconds away. We focused, we worked together with our paddles, and we attacked the next set of rapids with a determination that would make rocks tremble.

We progressed down the river for the next two hours, tackling one hazard after another, until we finally got a break and a chance to bask in the sun on the rocks.

I lay there, reflecting on what had been happening, and realized how the group in our raft, with its common goal in the face of adversity, was starting to become a team. We were not the best collection of athletes that day, but we were helping each other, listening to each other, trusting each other. Rolie was clearly the leader, with his incredible strength and technical knowledge of the river. John, who before today had been the flippant wiseacre, had become serious and focused. Duncan, who seemed to be a withdrawn thinker, had become a tower of strength in our raft. Ron, always the talker, was the steady, reliable influence, and I was finding myself caring that we worked together as a team.

After our half-hour break, we climbed back into our fragile raft to tackle the second half of this angry river. In a few minutes, we were going to discover what a real team will do.

We had been told about Seven Foot Falls, the most treacherous stretch of the whole river. As we dropped what seemed more like 20 feet from the top of the falls, Ron lost his balance and started to fall towards a rock called Deliverance. Without questioning, we pulled him back, not for a moment thinking whether we were risking our own stability. We weren't going to lose a team member. At the bottom of the falls, we went underwater hanging onto Ron, and then finally we emerged, very wet but very together.

We were the only team that day who did not lose someone into the Chattooga River. Our feeling of exhaustion and achievement when we finally floated across Lake Tugaloo to the shoreline is the feeling that real teams have. I still have our team photo from the end of that day. That experience welded us together in a way that is hard to describe. Working together for that common goal built a trust and a respect among one another and a pride in achievement which would be hard to destroy.

All this is about team building. You have to do this first. You don't have to ride the Chattooga River, but you do need to do something to give your team a sense of achievement and a better understanding of each other.

The next challenge is team operation, and the activity which is the biggest cause of wasted time in any organization: the meeting.

THE MEETING

The meeting is the ultimate focus of all team activity. It's where you come together to set your team's objectives, and plan how you are going to achieve those objectives. Meetings are also one of the greatest causes of wasted time and frustration in nearly all organizations. Most of this waste occurs because we don't plan and organize our meetings, and everyone assumes someone else is going to do the planning and organizing.

It's worth taking a moment to get clear on why we have meetings, and the factors that cause meetings to succeed or fail. Most organizations "have a meeting" when something goes wrong. You need to ask yourself whether your meeting is proactive or reactive. We often avoid the proactive meetings because we haven't got time, or because meetings are such bad experiences; the less of them, the better. This leads to far more reactive meetings later, and tends to develop an inner thinking in people that all meetings are problem-solving brainstorming sessions that get us out of today's crisis.

Getting back to those basic values of quality, we must be clear what output we require from a meeting, establish the input requirements from the participants, and apply prevention to the process by developing the skills, facilities, and procedures for the people involved in the meeting. Continuous improvement of the meeting process is driven by the participants' (or process owners') measuring the performance of the meeting.

We must also overlay these principles with a preventive reason for holding a meeting, and make our reasons proactive instead of reactive.

Putting these abstract ideas into practice means first identifying why we are having a meeting. If it was a crisis-driven reason, we must make one of the outputs of the meeting an action that will prevent this meeting from being held again. If it's not crisis-driven, then we are committed to planning ahead, and each person coming to the meeting needs to know the objectives of the meeting and what inputs they must bring. I'm reminded of Bob Bayette of ICI Paints, who said after six months in the quality process, "The biggest change experienced in the organization was that people no longer arrived at meetings saying 'What's this meeting about?'"

This means maintaining calendar integrity with your meetings (no last-minute changes) and issuing the agenda (generic agendas ought to be banned) with specific requirements for each item, at least three days before the meeting (more if you need it).

A meeting is held so that people can communicate information quickly and concisely. Once you have more than eight or nine people in your meeting, it is in danger of changing from a meeting into a conference.

The attendees all bring unique experiences and perspectives to a meeting. They must be able to speak with the authority of the department or activity they represent, and they must be committed to the objectives of the meeting. However, you need other components along with the technical or "process" elements of the meeting.

The team should have a blend of thinkers and doers. If you have a group of great "idea" people but no one to put those ideas into action, you'll have the common cause of failure for so many "technical committees," who deliberate for months and talk shop but don't implement. On the other hand, if you have a team that's all action people, it's like having a football team without any coaching staff. None of the moves are properly thought through, and jobs are duplicated or overlooked.

There is a third magic ingredient for a successful team. An old school colleague of mine, Peter Savage, wrote a book titled *Who Cares Wins*. You must have people on your team who care about the team, providing missing items like coffee and donuts and other equally vital special equipment you may need, as well as looking out for anyone who seems isolated and bringing them back in. Some would call this the "mothering" of the team. This caring should be shared among the team members.

Figure 16-1 (pages 188–191) shares a questionnaire your team members can complete. The questionnaire is reproduced from an excellent video called "Teams and Leaders," based on the work of Peter Honey (Melrose Learning Resources, publisher). It's well worth knowing if your team has a good balance of people, or whether you are all leaders, fighting each other for control of the team. When you've finished the questionnaire, use the score key that follows it to evaluate your individual profile as a team member. Take care when you complete the score key: the scores are to be entered in a different sequence than the questions themselves.

Having defined the outputs (objectives) and inputs (people and information) for your meeting process, you should next focus on the process itself. With the right inputs, you create the magic of synergy in your meeting when through trust and respect and overlapping frames of reference, the whole becomes greater than the sum of its parts. You move fast, you don't argue over small things, and team morale is outstanding.

Obstacles to Effective Meetings

I can hear you say, "This guy is in fantasy land; our meetings can never be like that." The obstacles to successful meetings arise because of lack of preparation, but we must first recognize the obstacles in order to eliminate them. All these obstacles lead to wasted time and frustration, so there's a real incentive to get rid of them.

Badly designed agendas (and not sticking to agendas, regardless of how good they are) are the biggest causes of failure in meetings. It's just like any other process in your business: you need a procedure to be followed in the meeting. Make the agenda specific, not generic, and issue it in time for people to prepare for their part of the meeting.

The next biggest problem is the other type of agenda: the hidden agenda. Having a well-designed agenda ahead of time enables the team to be ruthless about hidden agenda items. For those of you who haven't experienced the hidden agenda, it comes from one or two individuals at a meeting having objectives different from those of the team, and not revealing their objectives to the team. They usually try to disrupt the meeting by introducing unexpected information or some other crisis to throw the team off track, and then steer the team away from its objective. This is the worst disease a team can experience, and it must be stopped at its first symptoms.

Finally, the minutes of your team meeting must be lean and mean. They should just list decisions and actions, and never contain who said what to whom. No one ever reads that stuff. One page of minutes is the most you need for one or even two hours of a meeting.

You can use measurement to drive improvement in your meeting process. The check sheet in Figure 16-2 (page 192) is amazingly effective in telling you how to improve your meetings. As you get better, refine the check sheet and change the questions to be more specific, and drive *continuous* improvement.

Teamwork Questionnaire

This short questionnaire will help you discover your style when working in groups or teams. Throughout the questionnaire, imagine yourself as a member of a small group or team of six or so people. Simply read each item and decide as honestly as you can whether you often, sometimes, or rarely behave in the way described. Indicate whether it is often, sometimes, or rarely in the appropriate box beside each item.

	Often	Sometimes	Rarely
1. I go out of my way to encourage people in the group.	☐	☐	☐
2. I am inclined to get impatient with people who "beat around the bush."	☐	☐	☐
3. I urge the group to stick to plans and schedules, and meet deadlines.	☐	☐	☐
4. When there are different opinions within the group, I encourage people to talk their differences through to a consensus.	☐	☐	☐
5. I can be counted on to contribute original ideas.	☐	☐	☐
6. I use humor to ease tensions and maintain good relationships.	☐	☐	☐
7. I seek common understanding prior to making decisions.	☐	☐	☐
8. I listen carefully to what others have to say.	☐	☐	☐
9. I avoid getting involved in conflicts.	☐	☐	☐
10. I can quickly see what is wrong with unsound ideas put forward by others.	☐	☐	☐
11. I openly communicate the whys and wherefores of a situation.	☐	☐	☐
12. I am always ready to back a good suggestion in the common interest.	☐	☐	☐
13. I tend to put forward lots of ideas.	☐	☐	☐
14. I draw people out whenever I sense they have something to contribute.	☐	☐	☐
15. When things aren't progressing well, I push ahead and get the job done.	☐	☐	☐
16. I develop other people's ideas so they are improved.	☐	☐	☐
17. I tend to change my mind after listening to other people's points of view.	☐	☐	☐
18. I tend to seek approval and support from others.	☐	☐	☐

	Often	Sometimes	Rarely
19. I don't mind being unpopular if it gets the job done.	☐	☐	☐
20. I actively seek ideas and opinions from other people.	☐	☐	☐
21. I am a friendly person and find it easy to establish good rapport with others.	☐	☐	☐
22. I am careful not to jump to conclusions too quickly.	☐	☐	☐
23. I am good at noticing when someone in the group is feeling aggrieved or upset.	☐	☐	☐
24. I enjoy analyzing situations and weighing alternatives.	☐	☐	☐
25. I can work well with a very wide range of people.	☐	☐	☐
26. I have a reputation for using a no-nonsense "call a spade a spade" style.	☐	☐	☐
27. I like to feel I'm fostering good working relationships.	☐	☐	☐
28. I tend to be forceful and dynamic.	☐	☐	☐
29. I like to anticipate probable difficulties and be prepared for them.	☐	☐	☐
30. I press for action to make sure people don't waste time or go around in circles.	☐	☐	☐
31. I can usually get people to agree on a course of action.	☐	☐	☐
32. When people have second thoughts, I urge them to press on with the task at hand.	☐	☐	☐
33. I like to ponder alternatives before making up my mind.	☐	☐	☐
34. I tend to be open about how I'm feeling.	☐	☐	☐
35. People sometimes think I'm being too analytical and cautious.	☐	☐	☐
36. In discussions, I like to get straight to the point.	☐	☐	☐
37. While I'm interested in all views, I do not hesitate to make up my mind when a decision has to be made.	☐	☐	☐
38. Flippant people who don't take things seriously enough usually irritate me.	☐	☐	☐
39. I am able to influence people without pressuring them.	☐	☐	☐
40. I am able to think things through before doing something.	☐	☐	☐

Figure 16-1. Teamwork Questionnaire

Teamwork Questionnaire: Score Key

Item	Often	Sometimes
1		
4		
7		
8		
11		
14		
20		
31		
37		
39		

Total of items marked **often** [ ]

× 2 =

Total of items marked **sometimes** [ ]

Grand Total _____

LEADER

Item	Often	Sometimes
2		
3		
15		
19		
26		
28		
30		
32		
36		
38		

Total of items marked **often** [ ]

× 2 =

Total of items marked **sometimes** [ ]

Grand Total _____

DOER

Item	Often	Sometimes
5		
10		
13		
16		
22		
24		
29		
33		
35		
40		

Total of items marked **often** [ ]

× 2 =

Total of items marked **sometimes** [ ]

Grand Total _____

THINKER

Item	Often	Sometimes
6		
9		
12		
17		
18		
21		
23		
25		
27		
34		

Total of items marked **often** [ ]

× 2 =

Total of items marked **sometimes** [ ]

Grand Total _____

CARER

How to Score and Interpret Your Questionnaire

The questionnaire is designed to reveal your teamwork style and indicate which of the four roles you are best suited to. The four roles are:

Leader   Making sure that objectives are clear and agreed on and that everyone is involved and committed.

Doer   Urging the team to get on with the task at hand.

Thinker   Producing carefully considered ideas and weighing and improving ideas from other people.

Carer   Easing tensions and maintaining harmonious working relationships.

Which role or roles are you best suited to? It is possible that you are an all-arounder, equally at home with each of the four roles. Most people, however, have a role that fits best with their style, and another one or two roles that they can utilize if need be.

To score your questionnaire, indicate on the columns on the previous page which items you thought you did *often* or *sometimes*. Do not indicate items you marked as *rarely* done.

The maximum score for each role is 20. Your highest total score indicates the role you are best suited for. Your next highest indicates your backup role or roles. Low scores, say of 9 or less, suggest you are not comfortable with that particular role or roles. If your scores are all around the 15 mark, while you may prefer one or two roles, it suggests you are flexible enough to adopt any of the four roles.

Source: Trainer's Guide for "Teams and Leaders" video program (London: Melrose Learning Resources). Reprinted by permission.

Figure 16-1. Teamwork Questionnaire (continued)

Evaluating Your Meetings

One of the best ways of driving improvement is to measure performance. This meeting evaluation sheet will help you do this. All participants should complete the sheet and send the result to the chair or administrator. Keep score at the next meeting.

Meeting Evaluation	Yes	No
1. Was a clear agenda circulated beforehand?	☐	☐
2. Did the meeting start at the stated time?	☐	☐
3. Did everyone arrive before the meeting started?	☐	☐
4. Did more than half the people speak?	☐	☐
5. Did you complete the agenda with all actions settled?	☐	☐
6. Did you give adequate time to all items?	☐	☐
7. Did the meeting end on or before the agreed time?	☐	☐
8. Did the meeting help you in your work?	☐	☐
9. Did everyone get a minutes/action list within 24 hours?	☐	☐
10. Did you deal with all the top priority items?	☐	☐

Give one point for each "yes" answer.

0–3:   *You wasted a lot of people's time.*

4–6:   *Par for the course; tackle the weak points.*

7–8:   *Quite good; congratulate the organizer.*

9–10: *Exceptional; this meeting was a model to follow.*

Figure 16-2. A Meeting Evaluation Questionnaire

Chapters 13 through 16 have been about changes in people's behavior. The critical component in endorsing this change is recognition, which is the subject of Chapter 17.

BROWSER'S BRIEFING

- The skills of teamwork need to be developed in a practical (not theoretical) environment.
- Good leadership and good teamwork are inextricably linked.
- A good leader looks out for the needs of the team, and not just for his or her own needs.
- Build trust between team members by helping them overcome failure and by rewarding success.
- Understanding the background of other team members and giving training in interpersonal communication skills builds this trust and respect.
- Give a team a challenging but nonthreatening "nonwork" environment in which to operate. This will build trust.
- Have team members each discover whether they are doers, thinkers, or carers, in order to better understand their roles on the team.
- Meetings are the focal point of team activity and need to be managed with great care.
- All team members need to know the rules of your meetings, and you should all evaluate the effectiveness of your meetings, in order to drive meeting improvement.
- As with most activities, meetings succeed with good preparation.

17 Recognition

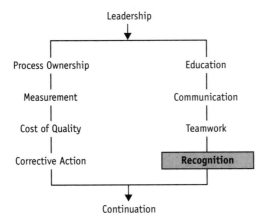

Some time ago, I was conducting an executive seminar with the board of Bell Mobility, the cellular phone division of Bell Canada. Just before lunchtime, we had been involved in a deep discussion about recognition, and in particular the power of peer recognition.

We broke for lunch, and as the vice presidents split into informal groups and chatted, the president, Bob Latham, walked purposefully towards me. He looked quite moved, and was quite intent about our discussion.

He then explained to me how the discussion about peer recognition had reminded him of the time, nearly 30 years previously, when he was an undergraduate and a member of the football team at Queen's University. It had been near the end of the season, and the team was out on the field practicing. He had captained the team that year, and they had had an exceptional season, winning nearly all of their games.

A number of the players were going on to play in the NFL and CFL, and would become great stars. This was a measure of the team's success.

As Bob practiced passing and catching with the team, one of the late arrivals ran over to him and asked, "Have you seen the notice board?"

"No," replied Bob, blankly.

"You've been elected Player's Player for the year!"

Nearly 30 years later, as president of a major organization, he still recalled the thrill that he felt with that news. He said, with great passion, "It is something I will remember all my life."

The power of recognition is something that too many companies overlook, and the reason for recognition is what few understand. Philip Crosby summed up what recognition is all about when he said, *"Appreciate those who participate."*

RECOGNITION AS A SOURCE OF CHANGE

If you want to change the values and the culture of your organization, recognition is the most powerful way of reinforcing the new behaviors the organization is seeking. Peer recognition is even stronger, and is the voice of everyone in the organization saying, "You did a great job."

You want to change from the values that say firefighters (who are actually the arsonists, remember?) will be rewarded, to values where people who consistently do it right the first time are recognized.

You want to change from a value where sitting on the status quo keeps people out of trouble to one where you recognize those people who are continuously improving their work processes, and are willing to take risks.

You have to start recognizing people who conform to customer requirements and are honest with the customer, instead of congratulating people who slipped something nonconforming past the customer when it didn't get noticed.

You need that clear picture, or vision, of the organization you are seeking to create, then relentlessly recognize the behaviors that you want to happen. Harvard Business School professor Rosabeth Moss Kanter wrote an excellent article on recognition, in which she said, *"People see pay or salary as a right. They see recognition as a gift."*

This is so true. We don't recognize people by giving them money. They just respond by saying, "I must have just done my job!" When you say thank you in special ways, they think, "I did something special; I'm going to do that again."

Other people see the recognition as well, and naturally emulate the behavior that has been endorsed.

However, to make recognition part of your culture, you need to decide at the outset what new values and behaviors you need to endorse. Where most go wrong is to believe that you simply throw recognition open to the newly "empowered" community of the organization. Surprise, surprise, recognition becomes hokey and devalued without a well-designed strategy. The recognition strategy has to be linked to the vision, culture, and values we discussed in Chapters 3, 4, and 5.

The leadership team must brainstorm at the outset the specific values it wants to endorse, and then recognize the behaviors that are based on these values. If bad housekeeping has been a major problem, then recognize good housekeeping. If late meeting starts are a problem, then recognize meeting chairs who start on time. If you see a problem getting people to do meaningful measurement, then recognize it.

However, recognition of your "good" practices must be supported by the rest of the people, and this is where the leadership then starts to draw in everybody else, collecting ideas on which "bad practices" must be eliminated and which "good practices" endorsed. You can't recognize everything, so decide what is important. Your list will be different from other organizations.

You won't be able to *measure* every "new behavior," but try to quantify success as much as possible, and remove subjectivity. In Chapter 16, we saw the meeting evaluation sheet. Use this to measure who runs the best meetings and you'll see that the chair is being evaluated by the peer group.

This brings us back to peer recognition. Without question, the more you build this into your recognition system, then the more you make change reach across the organization. You just saw the word *system* for the first time, and are perhaps thinking this is a cold and calculating procedure. Actually, it is a fun and happy activity, but above all, it must be seen as fair by everyone in the organization. That's why you must give everyone a system to work with. If you create the system, then spontaneous recognition will grow naturally.

DEVELOP A SYSTEM

So you must be systematic in developing recognition.

- Identify the values you want to endorse in your culture, e.g., conformance to requirements, prevention, process improvement, respect for the individual, etc.
- Define behavior you want to see that was not there in the past, and support these values, e.g., good housekeeping, sticking to procedure, delivering reports on time, etc.
- Measure performance of new behavior, but make it measurement by a group and not subjective, e.g., meeting evaluation, etc.

Now we come to the controversial part. *How* do we recognize the new behaviors? Remember the words of Rosabeth Moss Kanter, that people see payment as a right, and recognition as a gift. It's like finding a present for a good friend. Do they like books, are they the sporting type, or are they more domestic? Just because you like going to smart restaurants, doesn't mean that they will. Try to tailor the recognition to the person; this shows you care.

- A book on a subject that interests them; could you get it signed by the author?
- A box of golf balls with the person's name on them.
- A picture or memento for the home with a small "Thank You" plaque on it.
- If it is a meal out, give them something tangible as well that they will keep as a memento: a set of silverware, or monogrammed wine glasses…

What you don't do is give them an envelope with a check in it! That's just a bonus on the monthly paycheck.

The downside is that all of this means time and effort and actually caring about other people.

What sort of culture did you say you wanted?

These high-profile recognitions are the special items. They set the tone, but it is the day-to-day recognition which you want to happen just as much. Letters of recognition are the most powerful and memorable things people can receive. Being mentioned in a dispatch, to use the old military term, is something you should always remember for your team. I recall a letter I received back in 1968 from a boss I had at the time, Bruce Townsend. I was 3,000 miles from home, in the mountains of West Virginia in the middle of February, commissioning a chemical plant. It was tough, and Bruce took the trouble to write, rather than phone, and commend me. I could have handled anything from grizzlies to guns after that letter, and I continued to be prepared to travel anywhere in the world for that company. As an aside, he used a line in the letter which I've never forgotten: "The worst thing about experience is getting it!"

You've had letters like this one at some time in your career, and if you've ever had your name "mentioned in the dispatches," you know how you felt at the time. So, "do unto others as you would have them do unto you."

Staying with the idea of the thank-you letter, more about Bob Latham at Bell Mobility. Bob gave all the people in his organization the "tools" for the written thank-you. They all had a pad of "Bravograms" on their desk. If someone did something thoughtful or helpful for you, then at your fingertips was a Bravogram you could write to them to express your thanks. Philip Crosby did the same thing in his organization, and I remember seeing how people felt on receiving simple thank-you notes like the one in Figure 17-1. Don't forget to give people the tools as well as the framework for recognition.

Finally, you need to spend some time and effort looking at your basic pay and salary system. So many organizations design an excellent recognition system, but are then mystified as to why behavior didn't change. If you continue to pay people based on the old set of rewards, such as sales bonuses based on revenue, and not quality, then you will see that the sales people will continue to deliver revenue and not quality. Redesigning your basic pay system will need careful thought, and you should get an expert in the field to help you once you know what you want to reward.

Recognition is one of the most powerful activities in the change process. You need to treat it seriously, but make it the fun it deserves to be.

Bravogram!

To: Pat

Thank you for getting the monthly finance report here before lunchtime. Because of your prompt efforts, I've got an extra half day to work on the analysis, and can produce the more detailed analysis that was requested.

Regards, Chris

**Figure 17-1. A Thank-You Note
for Personal Recognition**

B R O W S E R ' S   B R I E F I N G

- Recognition is the way to reinforce the behaviors you want to encourage in your organization.
- Having the people of the organization, and not just the leadership, perform this recognition makes it all the more powerful.
- Behaviors are based on values. You all need to be clear on the values you want to endorse.
- *"People see pay or salary as a right. They see recognition as a gift."*— Rosabeth Moss Kanter
- As much as possible, you should measure behavior performance.
- Make the recognition memorable and appropriate to the individual or team.
- Invest time up front in researching and developing forms of recognition. (Remember benchmarking.)
- The recognition system must be consistent with your salary/reward system.

PART VI

THE CONTINUITY

18 | Continuation

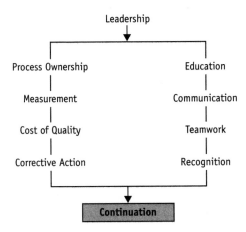

Entering a quality process is not unlike entering a marathon. If someone you know has run in a marathon, ask them what happens after 18 to 20 miles. Runners call it "The Wall." It is a physical and psychological phenomenon in which they feel that they have stopped moving forward. The effects are devastating. Runners prepare for the experience by "carbing up" and eating huge quantities of pasta before the race. Carbing up gives them extra physical reserves to get through the physical part of The Wall. Preparing for the psychological part of The Wall is more complex. The physical preparation is part of the psychological solution, but talking to other athletes and finding out about their experiences is also necessary. The runner needs techniques to strengthen mental powers, and above all to keep remembering the successes achieved so far. You've come 18 miles; there's only 8 to go. Think positively.

The principles are the same in the quality process. The energy to get through The Wall must come from constantly feeding people with knowledge and training to deal with their process challenges. The psychological strength comes from knowing what the successes have been, and quantifying those successes. Don't rename your quality process. If you feel like you're struggling, remember: renaming your quality process is like renaming your child after they come out of the "terrible twos." Don't rename your process if its been successful and met your objectives, and you're thinking of focusing on one particular area, such as process management or teamwork or ISO 9000. Make it clear that you are *focusing* and the other activities you have started will continue on as ever.

At first sight, a surprisingly large number of businesses enter their quality processes without a plan. As you look closer, you realize that it's not easy to plan for something you've never done before. Hindsight is 20/20, and a year down the track, so many companies say, "We wish we'd planned things better; we didn't realize how much time would be needed."

A second area where companies can run into trouble when they do make a plan is that they make their quality plan distinct from their business plan. When you make your business plan, the sales or customer budget is the driving force. When you make your quality plan, the customer *must* be the driving force. The plans may be separate initially, but they must ultimately be merged into one business plan, after the first year of your quality initiative at the latest.

PLANNING THE IMPROVEMENT PROCESS

So, how do you plan for something you've never done before? It's a bit like starting up a new business where you haven't yet got your first customer: you haven't developed the new product, but you know you've got a winning idea. One of the first things you do is look at other people. Talk to them about their experiences, ask them what they've learned, try to learn from their mistakes. It is a wise person who learns from his or her mistakes; it is a genius who learns from the mistakes of others. Try to be a genius!

You're truly looking at a start-up situation if it is your first time, but if you're trying to do it right the second time, then you need to go back and look at how much time and money and how many people have been involved in activities so far.

First-timers: ensure you keep really good records of time, money, and people involved in the quality process. This way, your next planning cycle, you will be so much more accurate. Remember, *you plan and manage quality in the same way you manage your finances.* So it's only like keeping expense receipts and supplier invoices.

The first thing to be planned is the vision and values activity. This work may be done in a weekend if your thoughts are well-developed, or it may take several months if you really want to go back to basics. Let's assume the vision and values activity is done over a period of about a month, and this has followed your initial self-assessment, using a first cut on your cost of quality.

If you look back through the preceding chapters, the ten elements of the change process have a "flow" to them; but perhaps you are unsure about how much time it will take to develop and implement each element.

A good way to regulate your activity in the early stages is to link it to your education plan. This is where the importance of just-in-time education starts to show. To give you a picture of how things will unfold, glance again through the timeline in Figure 18-1, then I'll talk you through it.

You can see that during the first three to six months, education (4) gives you a well-defined structure. However, don't think of it as education; think of it as a *well-defined use of the tools of quality.* So if this structure keeps you on track, why not continue with the well-defined use of the tools of quality after this initial education phase is completed? If you are restarting your quality process, then use your earlier education program to give this definition or structure to your restart. Use your management education to revisit the systems you designed and which may not be working satisfactorily, and use a facilitator or consultant to keep you on track.

Your employee education will probably have consisted of training in the use of process management tools and the development of teamwork and communication skills. Use this framework to tackle what you now know to be the process and people problems in the organization.

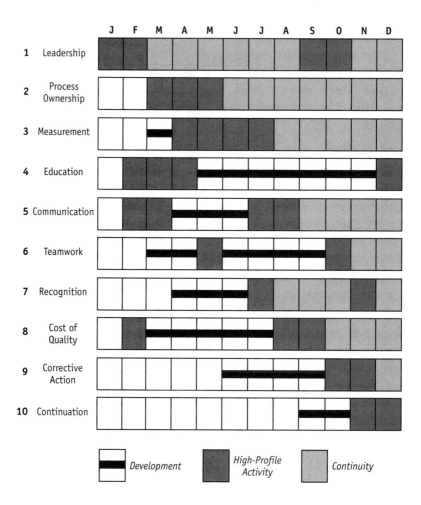

Figure 18-1. Implementation Timeline

The start-up (or restart) phase of your quality plan should begin with the leadership (1) commitment through your policy statement. The information from the first cut of cost of quality (8) and the mapping of business process flow (2) should be used to initiate mapping of problem processes. Widespread measurement (3) will probably commence after three to four months, and after six to nine months, you should be ready to feed this measurement data into your system for continuous cost of quality (8) collection. It is the cost of quality system that drives your corrective action (9) system, and you should have been process-proving your corrective action system during the three to nine month period. Once the cost of quality system is in place, you can link it to the corrective action system.

You will see that in parallel with developing your process management system, you need to be developing your communication (5) and recognition (7) systems, and teamwork (6) skills will be coming up to speed in time for full-scale operation of your corrective action (9) system.

It is often after this initial start-up phase driven by system design and intense education that the quality process starts to fade. The driving force was enthusiasm and evangelism, and the business leader typically turns the other way after nine months, thinking everything is self-sustaining. The next nine months shows a steady decline, and everyone wakes up after eighteen months to discover the process has stalled (see Chapter 22, "The New Organization").

Enthusiasm and evangelism are important, but they alone will not drive the quality process. The customer has to be the driving force, and your long-term quality plan has to be driven by the customer. All we have done so far is to make ourselves capable of being driven by the customer.

We must continue to work all the time on this capability. Don't assume that if you reach a certain capability you will automatically maintain it.

DRIVING THE QUALITY PLAN

The quality plan has to be driven by the current and future requirements of your key customers. In Chapter 2, I described a planning session with LePage Adhesives. They identified nearly 20 different interfaces for one "apparent customer." You should build a matrix like the one in Figure 18-2 showing your key clients by market segment, and for each client listing the "moments of truth," or client interfaces.

Identify your performance at each point in the matrix. Score out of 10 possible points, or if you're just feeling your way here, score out of 4. Avoid scoring out of 5; you'll have too many 3's!

When you've identified the most critical interfaces with the poorest performance, you need to look objectively at how the competition is

Market	#1			#2			#3		
Client	ACE Inc.	BOB Inc.	CAD Inc.	DAC Inc.	ELF Inc.	FX Inc.	GEC Inc.	HO Inc.	IBF Inc.
Buyer									
President									
Invoicing									
A/C Payable									
Receiving									
Technical									
Miscellaneous									

Figure 18-2. A "Moment of Truth" Matrix

doing, and you need to identify which of your business processes need to be improved to give the customer the performance they want. Benchmark your business processes against competitors, or even against customers and suppliers who have similar business processes, but which are working better than yours. Xerox Corporation, recognized as an initiator and leader of benchmarking, measured its processes against the following companies:

L.L. Bean: telephone response

American Express: invoicing

Ford: manufacturing layout

General Electric: robotics

This is the point at which you can now set your quality goals. Also, this is usually the point at which the *leadership* loses touch with the rest of the organization.

Goal setting is like budgeting, and you must involve the people who will achieve the goals in setting the goals. The tricky part is in identifying the resources needed; the time, money, and people required to meet your quality goals.

THE OLD ENEMY: TIME

You are looking to invest your time and energy to improve your business processes, and achieve a payback for both yourself and your customer. Cost of quality will give you some of the return you will get, but the big payoff is seen through increased customer satisfaction. If you're losing between $1 million and $3 million per year out of every $10 million of operating costs, or if people are wasting 10 to 15 hours per week reworking, handling complaints, or just plain "finding out the facts," then how much are you prepared to invest in people, time, and money to reduce this waste? I've already indicated that many Japanese companies have reached the point of investing 15 percent of their time, or six to eight hours a week, on continuous process improvement.

Most companies I work with feel at first so crisis-ridden and customer-driven that they can't think of sparing one hour a week to improve their customer service and product.

Your initial quality education will probably take two to three hours a week. I have seen so many companies get to the end of this, breathe a sigh of relief, and say, "Thank goodness; now we can get back to business as usual."

Instead, keep that momentum and continue to invest that time *every week* in continuous improvement activity. If you have a budget of ten hours a month, then a senior person might invest this as follows:

QMT meetings	*1 to 2 hours*
Departmental quality meetings	*2 hours*
Individual quality work with staff	*2 to 3 hours*
Work alone on process improvement	*2 hours*
Cross-functional corrective action team	*2 hours*

Compare this with:

Lunch	*20 hours* *(per month)*

And other individuals in the organization would budget their time differently:

Department quality meeting	*2 hours*
Individual quality work with a manager	*½ hour*
Work alone on process improvement	*2 hours*
Cross-functional corrective action teams	*5 to 6 hours (per month)*

You can see that the manager needs to be looking at more than 10 hours a month, and that 15 hours a month, or three to four hours per week, is probably more realistic.

It is critical to budget your time investment as well as your money investment. You then need to make decisions as to where you are under-resourced, either in numbers of people or skills, and make your decisions on obtaining external resourcing in consulting, training, or other services.

The goals you set must be challenging, and you must be clear on the return you expect over the next year, two years, and five years. You can see how this whole process starts to integrate with the strategic planning for your whole business.

Measuring your process (assessment) is an important part of continuation, and in short, you need to think about continuously improving your continuous improvement process. You will recall measurement (or assessment) is the driving force for process mapping.

You now need a method for assessing this plan and the quality process, and that is the subject of Chapter 19.

BROWSER'S BRIEFING

- People pursuing the quality process can "hit The Wall," just as a marathoner often does at the 18-mile mark.
- Breaking through The Wall requires preparation: giving people the knowledge and training to meet their challenges.
- It's not easy to plan something you haven't done before, so look at how other people have done it.
- Record your successes and failures, as well as time, money, and people usage, during the first year (and subsequently) so that you can continuously improve your continuous improvement.
- Initially, your quality plan may be separate from your business plan, but they *must* eventually be merged.
- Build a timeline for each of the elements of the change process.
- In the early stages, most of your activities will be structured around your education, so use this as the defining element.
- Design of quality systems, such as cost of quality, corrective action, communication, and recognition, will also be defining factors.
- The quality plan is driven by the requirements of your customers. So is your business plan, which is why the two must merge.
- Careful recording of time invested in your quality activities will enable your future planning to be more effective.
- You should evaluate the effectiveness of your quality plan.

19 Using the Baldrige Criteria to Assess Quality Systems

In the early 1980s, U.S. industry was being "taken to the cleaners" by the Japanese, and the Secretary of Commerce, Malcolm Baldrige, saw the need for a government initiative to strengthen the competitive edge of business. This was at a time when President Ronald Reagan was reducing government involvement in all aspects of national life. However, Baldrige shared a common interest in horse riding with Reagan, and used these opportunities when they rode together to persuade Reagan to adopt a government initiative.

The U.S. National Quality Award was developed by bringing together businesses such as IBM and Xerox, consulting practices such as Philip Crosby Associates and the Juran Institute, and professional associations such as the American Society for Quality Control. Together they built a methodology for assessing the "quality maturity" of organizations. Today it is generally recognized as the most comprehensive form of organizational assessment yet developed.

Sadly, Malcolm Baldrige, the prime mover in this development, was killed in an accident just as the development work was coming to completion. As a tribute to his drive and initiative, the U.S. National Quality Award was named for him when it was first given in 1987. The Baldrige Award is managed by the National Institute of Standards and Technology and administered by the American Society for Quality Control. The award was restructured for its tenth anniversary in 1997, with a goal of providing a better systems perspective for performance management.

A company that has decided to embark on a journey of quality improvement needs to have a plan. The Baldrige assessment process measures the *effectiveness* of a company's quality improvement plan. The action plans guide the overall direction of the company to ensure customer satisfaction and market success. The system is the means for delivering on that plan.

CATEGORIES OF THE BALDRIGE CRITERIA

The Baldrige Award's 1997 Criteria for Performance Excellence look at a company's quality system in seven categories:

1. Leadership

2. Strategic Planning

3. Customer and Market Focus

4. Information and Analysis

5. Human Resource Development and Management

6. Process Management

7. Business Results

Figure 19-1 gives a graphic depiction of how these elements relate in the 1997 criteria. First, the system must be management driven, and Category 1, Leadership, assesses how a company is led along its quality journey. However, this leadership has to be customer driven, as you can see from the position of Category 3, Customer and Market Focus, in the figure. The leadership must create a Strategic Plan, Category 2, to achieve the customer satisfaction that leads to business success.

The deployment of the Strategic Plan is achieved through the balanced development of Human Resource Development and Management, Category 5, and Process Management, Category 6. This balance between people and processes has been the focus of Parts IV and V of this book.

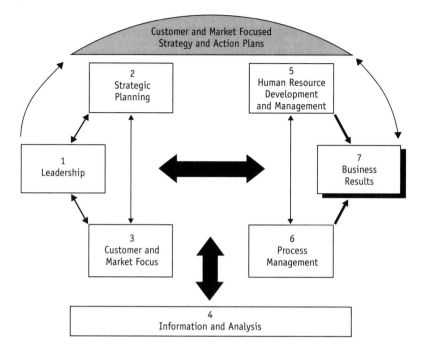

Figure 19-1. 1997 Baldrige Award Criteria Framework—A Systems Perspective

Successful deployment of the plan produces the Business Results, Category 7. These six categories constitute the system, which is in turn supported by Information and Analysis, Category 4.

An organization that is reactive in its quality approach will score up to 400 points. An organization with a truly prevention-based system of operation can score in the region of 500 points. To be world class (800 points or more) in quality approach and deployment requires a company to show:

• A sound, systematic approach

• A fact-based improvement process, with evidence of refinement and improved integration as a result of improvement cycles and analysis

• A well-deployed approach that may vary in some areas but has no major gaps (1997 Baldrige Award Criteria)

A Baldrige assessment will cause you to see the need for improvement from a strategic perspective, and you may well endorse some of your cost of quality findings, such as poor communication.

Another method of assessing your organization is through ISO 9000. I have seen the look of horror on the faces of those who have tried to read the international standard on quality. Company presidents give up quickly, and dump the document on the poor quality manager. However, your favorite and biggest customer may be saying to you that in two years' time, they will stop buying from you if you haven't become ISO 9000 registered. You can use the ISO 9000 audit as a way of assessing your organization at a more operational level than Baldrige.

Sadly, many organizations miss the value of the ISO standards at the start. They see them as an unnecessary cost, requested by an unreasonable and even inefficient customer. They fail to see that ISO assessment can give a real insight into the opportunities for improvement inside an organization. Teamed up with process improvement it can become a powerful force to drive business improvement. We'll revisit ISO 9000 in Chapters 20 and 21.

Assessment of your organization using either cost of quality analysis, Baldrige criteria, or ISO 9000 will tell you at the outset where improvements are needed and how big your opportunity is. Later on, assessment will be the driving force to continuously improve your Continuous Improvement Process.

So first of all, we'll look at Baldrige assessment, examining each category of the performance excellence criteria in more detail.

(CATEGORY 1)

LEADERSHIP

Right at the outset, the criteria ask how the senior executives guide the company and develop their leadership. If executives (the top people in the organization) only make speeches and hand out awards, this category will be scored very low. Do they seek out new business opportunities for the company? What are the values or principles on which the leaders operate, and do they communicate these values? Are their actions based on the quality values of the organization? If the organization has a value of "conforming to customer requirements," do the leaders themselves conform to the internal and external customer requirements in their daily activities? This reveals rapidly whether leaders are doing more than merely talking a good game. Which business processes are they measuring? What personal development do they undergo each year? What percentage of time is spent on these things? Actions speak louder than words.

The other action that is evaluated is whether leaders communicate these values to organizations outside the company, and to the community. Does the company involve itself in the outside community in which it operates, or is it just an island in isolation? This can mean involvement with professional bodies, charitable organizations, or community organizations. Are people "told" to do this, or does the company support this activity? Is the company genuinely outward-looking? How does the company evaluate its impact on the community, from the product or service it delivers to the operation of its facilities or processes?

In Category 1, a company can score a maximum of 110 points out of the total 1,000 points. A typical organization might pull together 40 or 50 points here.

(CATEGORY 2)

STRATEGIC PLANNING

Next is Category 2, Strategic Planning, which must be shown to be developed by the leadership as a result of listening to the customer. As we get deeper into the next categories, we are also going to see the importance of *linkage* between each of the categories.

The score for Strategic Planning is 80 out of 1,000 points. It is critical, as it is linked to both Customer and Market Focus (Category 3), and Leadership (Category 1). Strategic Planning must also be shown to be based on management by fact (Category 4, Information and Analysis) and involvement of people (Category 5, Human Resource Development and Management), and to depend on capable processes (Category 6, Process Management).

The key issue here is that the Strategic Planning must be integral with the business plan, and not a superficial component. This category is a *core* category.

The whole planning process has to be shown to be customer driven, which is of course what happens with a good business plan anyway. But preparing the plan is not enough. You must show how the plan is deployed into the organization, how resources are drawn in to make the plan happen, and how progress is monitored. This is where Figure 19-1 shows a linkage across to Categories 5, 6, and 7.

The Strategy Plan must contain projections for the next two to five years. It must show the strategies for achieving the objectives, together with the resources that will be required. The longer-term objectives need to show the significant improvements in performance that will be achieved, and compare these with the main competitors' performance. A properly constructed plan with the right inputs produces Business Results (Category 7), which have not occurred by accident.

(CATEGORY 3)

CUSTOMER AND MARKET FOCUS

This category formerly included the item of Customer Satisfaction and was worth 250 points in the scoring. In the 1997 criteria, the Customer Satisfaction Results item (130 points) and the Market Results item were placed in Category 7, Business Results. The Customer and Market Focus category is now worth 80 points.

This category is primarily about how you communicate with the customer. How do you identify customer requirements, both now and for the future? These requirements need to be understood for each market segment, and the collection process has to be clearly defined. The process for determining the relative importance of requirements must also be defined, and both of these processes must be the focus of continuous improvement.

Customer relationships through telephone, letter, and personal contact need to be both outgoing and incoming. Customers need to be contacted in the important after-sale period to establish satisfaction.

Customer communication must be effective, and the technology to enable the best customer contact must be provided.

In the event of customer dissatisfaction, how are these problems resolved, and more importantly, how is the customer feedback used to drive process improvement and skills development? How is the information drawn together and analyzed? At the same time, how does the company ensure that complaints are resolved promptly?

All of the information produced by customer contact must be analyzed to enable Strategic Planning (Category 2). This leads us conveniently into the next category.

(CATEGORY 4)

INFORMATION AND ANALYSIS

This category is about measurement. How do you determine what to measure? Are the things you measure important to the customer, do you use the data to drive improvement, and are you systematic in selecting your measurements? This category embraces all the other categories in the framework and counts for 80 points.

We talked a lot about measurement in earlier chapters, and the examiners are going to look at how you choose what to measure. A lot of companies measure everything, but when you ask what they do with the information, they'll say, "It goes into a report."

Your primary measurement must be in marketplace performance, and must occur at the primary impact point, or "moment of truth" with the customer. You should then be measuring at key points back up the process chain, to ensure that your internal processes are under control. You need to select the critical few points at which to measure. The measurement itself must be objective, and measurement data is notorious for being subjective. How many times do you hear, "The customer doesn't know what they want!"?

There is an important ring of truth here. Customers will tell you where you are going wrong, but often can't tell you what delivery time they really need, or what type of service they require, simply because they don't know the capability of your processes.

Having selected what you are going to measure, the next question is how to ensure that the method of measurement is accurate. This links back to objectivity. We all know how unreliable those hotel "happiness sheets" are—the customer is asked for feedback, but the feedback does not come from a representative profile of clients. In manufacturing, calibration of the data collection instrument is the critical issue. If you are collecting information reliably, are you then delivering it to the people who will act on the information? Or is it going into those unread reports? How do you know what is a good or a bad result in your measurement? Are you benchmarking your processes against similar processes in other organizations you recognize as "best of breed"?

Finally, having got the information, what do you do with it? This is the crunch. How is the information analyzed and then how are the results compared with your projections?

Once you identify the need for change, how do you make it happen? You need a systematic approach—a corrective action system, a cost of quality system, and maybe others as well. And how about a system for improving your systems!

Clearly, data is a critical input to your Strategic Plan, but remember the importance of keeping a balance between process and people as you deploy that plan.

(CATEGORY 5)
HUMAN RESOURCE DEVELOPMENT AND MANAGEMENT

The items addressed here include Work Systems; Employee Education, Training, and Development; and Employee Well-Being and Satisfaction. These are a lot of issues for one category, and it scores 100 points.

You need to show that you are planning your people requirements over the next two to five years, to show linkage to Strategic Planning (Category 2). You must also show how you plan to develop the people you already have. Not surprisingly, this plan has to be supported by hard data, and not by "guesstimates."

Having set your plan, how do you involve the people? Do you encourage teamwork? Do you have a communication system? Are people owning their processes and making decisions, or do you still have a hierarchy of baby-sitters? Do you encourage initiative? Again, how do you *measure* the involvement?

As people become more involved and your organization thinks further ahead, your educational needs will grow. How do you assess these needs, and how do you measure the existing skills and knowledge? How do you analyze the gap, and how do you close it? You need to have a plan for delivering quality education and training, not just to new people but to people in existing jobs where their processes may be changing more rapidly. Not surprisingly, measurement of this activity is essential—not just measurement of what you give people, but measurement of how *effective* the delivery is.

In this changing environment, we've already seen the importance of performance measurement, which gives people feedback on how they are doing, and recognition, as confirmation of that feedback. The assessment will evaluate these areas.

If you're doing these things in the right way, the effects on your employee education and morale should be significant. You should also be looking at health and safety issues and work environment, and these of course feed back into strengthening well-being and morale. This whole quality business is about change, continuous change. How do you equip people to handle change? Yet again, how do you measure their morale and well-being?

The output of all these efforts is products and services which meet customer requirements, and these lead into Process Management.

(CATEGORY 6)
PROCESS MANAGEMENT

This category looks at how you design your products and services, how you control your delivery processes from initial request to final receipt, and whether you measure the effectiveness of these processes and improve them continuously. Do you keep records of both how to operate processes and their performance in operation? All these principles need to be applied to your business or administrative activities as well as your operations; none of them will be fully effective unless you are also using these principles in your dealings with your suppliers and business partners.

The content of this category is worth up to 100 points.

Whether you are talking "hard product" or "service product," the principles are the same. And if you've done ISO 9000 work, you'll find that this whole category will come a lot easier.

It all starts with design and ensuring that the customer's requirements become part of the design, not conveniently ignored. Your design should be within the capability of your operation to produce, and within the capability of your suppliers to be a resource. The whole design function should be the focus of continuous improvement activity, and also be subject to continual reduction in cycle time.

Once you've got it clear what the customer wants, you must have processes which are capable of delivery, and this capability must be assessed by measurement. If the evidence from measurement shows processes are not in control, you need to have a methodology for root cause analysis. And you even need to be evaluating the reliability of your measurements!

The natural outcome is then to improve the process, using the data from measurement. You need to show that you have the process in place, including a methodology to show which processes you select for improvement.

The organization's systems, processes, practices, and products need to be assessed internally, which will be routine for ISO 9000 registered companies, and the information from these assessments used for process measurement.

Recording of procedures and results is another routine activity for ISO 9000 registered companies, but this recording should also be the subject of continuous improvement.

All of this activity is normally applied to operational activity, but needs also to be applied to business processes, such as finance, marketing, personnel, legal, and purchasing.

Supplier quality is the last area to be addressed in this category. Too many companies ignore their suppliers in process management. You must show evidence of clear communication of requirements to suppliers, and auditing of suppliers' own processes. You must show evidence

Portland Center Library
George Fox University
12753 SW 68th St.
Portland, OR 97223

Thu Sep 23 1999

Judy A Edwards
5046 NE Farmcrest
Hillsboro OR 97124

PAGING SLIP

A request has been placed for the following item by the patron indicat
Please retrieve the requested item from the stacks.   Fold the pagin
slip, place it in the book and take the book to the Circulation
Department and place on "Shelves for Paged Items."

LOCATION: MLRC:Main Stacks
PICKUP AT: PCL Circulation Desk

30:5

of development of suppliers and partners, and a clear strategy in supplier and partner selection and development.

This takes us to the last Baldrige category, the final outcome of the organization's effort: Business Results.

(CATEGORY 7)

BUSINESS RESULTS

In the updated Criteria for Performance Excellence, the Business Results category scores 450 points, the biggest by far. This is where you show the results of your efforts, and the linkage of cause and effect must be clear. You will achieve a high score only if you can show that the results are linked to the activities in Categories 1 through 6. Many companies have good quality results through good luck. This won't suffice, because good luck and bad luck wash out in the long term. This category must also show a linkage to Category 3, Customer and Market Focus. "Good" quality results are only relevant if they are results that matter to the customer.

The actual measurement of customer satisfaction and market share needs to focus on individual customer groups, and then be compared with levels achieved by competitors. Further comparison with customer complaint data should be used to validate data. Positive trends in customer satisfaction also must be shown.

Your quality results must also be compared with those of your main competitors. Market share, business growth, and marketplace performance must show how you fit in the "big picture."

Financial performance has been introduced to the Business Results category to identify the enterprise's return on economic value.

Digging deeper into your organization, you must also show results in employee development, and this will link to Category 5, Human Resource Development and Management.

You need to show improvement in your supplier and partner performance, and again compare these results with your competitors' performance.

Finally and most significantly company-specific results account for 130 points—on a par with the Customer Satisfaction and Financial and Market Results items in this category. These company-specific results are your key performance indicators and will only show after two or three years of effort. This is why your organization must be managed by fact, in order to produce results that are not just good luck. This takes us back to Category 4, Information and Analysis, which is the foundation for all other categories in the Baldrige criteria.

CRITICISM OF THE BALDRIGE FRAMEWORK

There is no question that the Baldrige assessment is extensive, comprehensive, and exhaustive. You finish with the feeling that no quality stone has been left unturned. The exhaustive (or exhaustion) aspect has often caused criticism. The 1997 revision has responded by reducing the number of individual business areas to be addressed from 52 to 30.

Criticism also comes from people who feel nominations should be made by customers and not by the potential winners themselves. Some people think the criteria are too "internally" focused and insufficiently customer focused. However, 530 of the 1,000 points come from Business Results and Customer and Market Focus, and these can only come from happy customers.

Other criticism comes from the lack of financial analysis of a company's performance; many cite the difficulties experienced by the Wallace Company after winning the award. The 1997 response has been to include Financial Results as an item of the Business Results category. Baldrige Award winners are expected to serve as advocates for the award during the year after winning. Small companies like Wallace have difficulty finding the resources to do this without adversely affecting the running of the business.

The other major change in the 1997 Baldrige guidelines is a strong shift toward strategic thinking and systems thinking, and detractors will accuse the award criteria of following popular fashion.

Having said all of this, the Baldrige Award framework is still the benchmark when it comes to assessment of quality improvement processes. Nevertheless it can be intimidating for beginners in quality— one reason many are turning to ISO 9000 as a more basic way of assessing an organization's quality activity. That is the subject of Chapter 20.

BROWSER'S BRIEFING

- It is imperative to measure the effectiveness of your quality plan.
- Assessment using the criteria of the Baldrige Award is the most comprehensive method available.
- The Baldrige approach assesses an organization on its Leadership, Strategic Planning, Customer and Market Focus, Human Resource Development and Management, Process Management, and Business Results, all supported by Information and Analysis.
- Organizations score up to 1,000 points, depending on their quality "maturity."
- Reactive organizations may score around 400 points. World class organizations score in the 800-point range.
- *Leadership* needs to show that they are listening to the customer, and are truly practicing quality in their daily actions.
- *Strategic Planning* is directly linked to Leadership and to Customer and Market Focus.
- *Customer and Market Focus* demonstrates a company's knowledge of the market and its system for determining and communicating customer requirements.
- *Information and Analysis* needs to show that you "manage by fact," and also that you choose carefully what you will measure.
- *Human Resource Development and Management* covers a wide range of issues, including Work Systems; Employee Education, Training, and Development; and Employee Well-Being and Satisfaction; it needs to be planned for the coming two to five years.
- *Process Management* analyzes how you see your products through from start to finish.
- The expanded *Business Results* category includes customer satisfaction and financial results, as well as human resource, supplier/partner, and company-specific results. These results must be shown to come from the business plan created by the leadership having listened to the customer. Happy accidents do not score well.
- The Baldrige framework is comprehensive, but for some it may be too much. ISO 9000 is often used as a "starter kit" for companies just beginning in quality.

20 | ISO 9000

In World War II the war machines of the various nations, remembering the chaos of World War I, initiated the widespread military practice of assessing suppliers for reliability and quality. They needed a way of ensuring that suppliers produced weapons that operated right *the first time*. The leaders would not allow the risk of ammunition that only worked *most* of the time.

The military developed performance standards for their suppliers, and inspectors audited factories for an "assurance" that the manufacturer was capable of operating their processes in a reliable and consistent manner. The principles of process analysis and process management were developed, and became the basis for postwar standards on quality assurance.

After World War II, industry saw the value of the military standards on quality assurance. If a company could audit a supplier's processes and evaluate whether these processes were definable, repeatable, and predictable, then the supplier was "in control," and could be relied on to deliver goods or services that conformed to requirements.

Various national standards were developed through the 1970s. The British Standard BS5750, the United States Standard Q90, and the Canadian Standard Z299 became prototype national quality standards.

During the 1980s, as business became global and nations recognized the value of an international standard, the concept of ISO 9000, the international standard on quality, was conceived.

ISO 9000 is much misunderstood. Some sages of total quality say that it is old-fashioned and out-of-date in its approach. Company presidents say it's expensive, and why pay out tens of thousands of dollars for something which does not get delivered to the customer? Company managers fear a bureaucracy of manuals.

The good news is that ISO 9000 doesn't have to be any of these things. It can drive down your operating costs by as much as 10 percent, by forcing you to be more disciplined about your business processes. Steve MacCowski will tell you how Firmin Coates, a trucking contractor to Shell U.K., have reduced their insurance premiums by 17 percent through ISO 9000 registration. It can also be a great marketing tool to attract new customers (and retain old ones). Finally, it is something that forces you to take action if you want certification. To become certified (or registered) to an ISO 9000 standard, you have to meet the requirements in the standard, in itself a great discipline, because an external auditor comes in to review whether you have met the standard's requirements. The auditor will also check whether you have managed to avoid a bureaucracy of manuals.

Think of ISO 9000 like a driver's license. You are simply going back to driving school to get rid of those bad driving habits you developed over the years. If examiners see that you have done that, they will give you a certificate to prove it. You can then show the certificate to customers as evidence that you are safe to drive your business on their territory. They have an assurance that your business processes are definable, repeatable, and predictable. There is much less chance of your letting them down.

THE DRIVING FORCE BEHIND ISO 9000

Contrary to popular belief, the driving force behind ISO 9000 is not the International Organization for Standardization in Geneva; the driving force behind ISO 9000 is your company's customers. Your customer wants an assurance that you will deliver what you have promised. The IOS has produced the ISO 9000 series of standards as a method for customers to identify whether their suppliers have a quality system capable of delivering what they have promised. The standards are largely based on the principles of process management. Incidentally the word ISO is derived from the Greek word *isos* meaning "the same."

The ISO 9000 standard contains a series of requirements which have to be met. If an organization can meet these requirements, then it can be certified as meeting the requirements of the ISO 9000 standard. The requirements of the standard all focus in turn on the ability of a supplier to meet the requirements of its customer. Up to 20 requirements must be met. One example of these requirements is that for contract review, which says, *"Before submission of a tender or acceptance of a contract or order, the tender, contract, or order shall be reviewed to ensure ... the supplier has the capability to meet contractual or accepted order requirements."*

A successful third-party audit of an organization's processes leads to the granting of a certificate or registration—like the driver's license I referred to earlier.

We need to understand the concepts of quality and process management to understand how ISO 9000 operates.

ISO 9000 AND PROCESS MANAGEMENT

From earlier chapters, you will recall that all organizations consist of a series of processes that link together to deliver a product or service to an external customer. Each process must be the responsibility of someone in the organization. All these processes need to link together smoothly if we are going to deliver reliably to our customer (see Figure 20-1). ISO 9000 requires processes to be audited to see if they operate smoothly. However, the final arbiter on whether you have delivered quality is the customer.

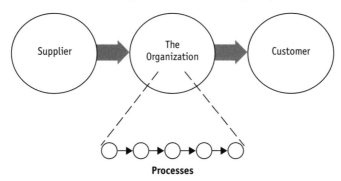

Figure 20-1. The Role of Processes in the Supply Chain

The ISO 9000 audit will evaluate whether you are capable of meeting the customer's requirements.

THE ISO 9000 REQUIREMENTS

The standard defines either 16, 19, or 20 requirements for your business, depending on the scope of certification you want for your business. ISO 9003 is the narrowest scope of certification, and defines 16 areas. ISO 9002 is the most frequently obtained scope of certification, and defines 19 areas. ISO 9001 is the widest scope, with 20 areas, but certification takes much longer and costs much more to achieve than for ISO 9002. The list below shows you the categories requiring certification if you go for ISO 9001. I'm going to ignore ISO 9003; less than 5 percent of companies go for it, and as customers understand more about the standard, they'll be less likely to accept ISO 9003.

When you first look at the 20 requirements of ISO 9001, it's like sitting down to a five-course meal with each component of each course strung out in a long line—but not necessarily in the order you would eat them. Imagine a menu that reads paté, ice cream, fish, toast, broccoli, etc., and appears to have no structure. Actually, there is a logic in the flow of the requirements, but the standard does not immediately reveal it. In Figure 20-2, I have broken the 20 components of ISO 9001 into five "courses," and tried to disrupt as little as possible the flow of the requirements. I've pulled out of sequence Internal Quality Audit (4.17) and Statistical Techniques (4.20), because I see them as relating to the Organization grouping and the Inspection and Correction grouping, respectively. You could also argue that Document and Data Control (4.5) and Quality Records (4.16) fit in other groups, but the case is not as strong. (Incidentally, I prefer to call the ISO 9000 requirements "Categories," as this causes less confusion when we start talking about customer requirements.)

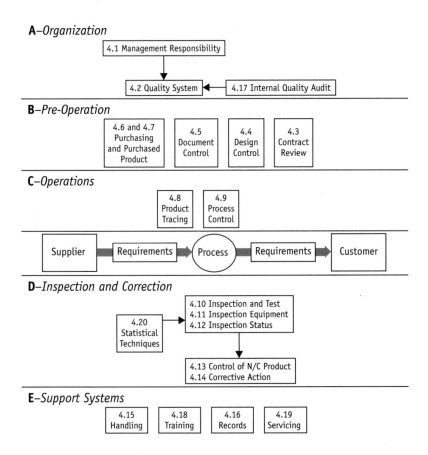

A–*Organization*

4.1 Management Responsibility

4.2 Quality System ◄─── 4.17 Internal Quality Audit

B–*Pre-Operation*

| 4.6 and 4.7 Purchasing and Purchased Product | 4.5 Document Control | 4.4 Design Control | 4.3 Contract Review |

C–*Operations*

| 4.8 Product Tracing | 4.9 Process Control |

| Supplier | ⇒ Requirements ⇒ | Process | ⇒ Requirements ⇒ | Customer |

D–*Inspection and Correction*

4.20 Statistical Techniques ─►
4.10 Inspection and Test
4.11 Inspection Equipment
4.12 Inspection Status

4.13 Control of N/C Product
4.14 Corrective Action

E–*Support Systems*

| 4.15 Handling | 4.18 Training | 4.16 Records | 4.19 Servicing |

Figure 20-2. Categories of ISO 9001 Requirements

THE QUALITY MANUAL

The ISO standards require that *"The supplier shall establish, document and maintain a Quality System as a means of ensuring that product conforms to specified requirements."*

The quality manual is the focus of most of the activity in achieving ISO 9000 certification. There are four "layers" in the manual. Because the content increases as you get deeper into the manual, the structure is shown as a pyramid in Figure 20-3.

**Figure 20-3. Four Layers of the
Quality Manual**

The *policy manual* assembles the policy statement for each of the 19 or 20 categories for which you require certification. It will be probably be 25 to 30 pages in length, and should be a document you would be happy to give any customer. You should make this a showpiece. This manual should rarely need updating, and should be a true statement of policy, not a wish list. Try to keep it concise; the challenge is to avoid including procedures. A concise manual is a sign to the auditor that you have taken care in its preparation. I'm reminded of a story attributed to the great playwright George Bernard Shaw, and also to the French philosopher Pascal. Shaw was a great letter writer, and he had once spent the best part of a day writing a letter to a friend. At the end of the letter he paused, reflected, and wrote, "I'm sorry this letter is so long, I didn't have time to write a short one." Food for thought!

Shaw's words will apply even more to the *procedure manual*. Here, you will document each of the steps you go through to execute a process. Well-written procedures are concise and understandable. They will be a working document, which anyone should be able to pick up and use when doing a job. As with the policy manual, the best person to write the procedure manual is the process owner. The key to success is to have your people know how to write a policy or procedure, and then have manuals which truly reflect the practice in your business. An outsider can never write the best procedures for you.

The procedure manual will need constant updating as your processes change, and the Document Control section of the standard confirms this: *"The supplier shall establish and maintain documented procedures to control all documents and data that relate to the requirements of this International Standard."*

A copy of the operating procedures that relate to a department needs to be kept in that department, and the procedures need to be cross-referenced with the appropriate section in the policy manual. Keeping control on the procedure and policy manuals is a critical task.

The next layer in the manual is the *work instructions*. These are the instructions for performing each task in the business, and are simply a detailed breakdown of the procedural activity.

Finally, *forms, tags, and labels* means you need to catalog these items for the whole business. This will be a great opportunity for better housekeeping in the organization.

AUDITING THE QUALITY SYSTEM

The manual you build must be a true statement of practice. Before you go for certification, you need to audit your own quality system, and the standard even requires you do this. The Internal Quality Audit requirement states that *"The supplier shall establish and maintain documented procedures for planning and implementing of internal quality audits to verify whether quality activities and related results comply with planned arrangements, and to determine the effectiveness of the quality system."*

In your manual, *you say what you do.* The challenge is to ensure that throughout the organization, *you do what you say.* You prove this to an auditor by *recording what you did.*

There is also a requirement of the standard called quality records, which states *"The supplier shall establish and maintain documented procedures for identification, collection, indexing, filing, storage, maintenance and disposition of quality records."* Thus, you can see the importance of having everyone in the organization understanding their role in achieving certification, and in keeping reliable records of activity.

The internal audit will reveal discrepancies which can be corrected, and you should then set about selecting an auditor for registration. A qualified registrar will be accredited by an accreditation body such as the Standards Council of Canada, the Registrar Accreditation Board (RAB) in the United States, or the National Accreditation Council for Certification Bodies (NACCB) in the United Kingdom. Each of these organizations will supply an up-to-date list of the registrars who can audit for ISO 9000.

When selecting a registrar, you need to check for such things as "Memoranda of Understanding," to ensure that your registration will be recognized in other countries. Waiting periods and costs are obvious things to check for, and the reputation of a proposed auditor can be checked against previous organizations they have audited. The most important consideration is that the registration with your chosen auditor will be recognized by your customer who is asking you to be certified.

The auditor should be a body you feel comfortable working with. The final audit will be about four to five days in length, but there will be preparation time with the auditor, and if you achieve certification, the auditor will be carrying out surveillance audits every six months during the three years that your certification is valid. At the end of three years, you will need to undergo a full reaudit.

KEYS TO SUCCESS

Most important is commitment by the senior management of the organization. The very first requirement in the ISO 9000 standards, Management Responsibility, requires that *"The supplier's management with executive responsibility shall define and document its policy for quality, including objectives for and commitment to quality."* It also requires that *"The quality system ... shall be reviewed at appropriate intervals by the supplier's management."* Delegating the task to a quality manager is not a road to success.

Having the management team write each of the policies relevant to their part of the business ensures commitment and involvement, and having the procedures be written by the process owners ensures ownership of the manual. When the policies and the procedures are written, you should ensure they are a true statement of practice, not a "wish list."

Finally, remember George Bernard Shaw's words, and take the time to write a short manual. Be concise!

WHERE DO WE GO FROM HERE?

Educating the management team is the first critical step. It probably requires about two days of work as a team. They will then understand the scope of ISO 9000 appropriate for the business, and they will understand the 19 or 20 requirements which have to be met. This work should be led by a person who is conversant with the ISO 9000 standards. The team can then make decisions and plan on the issues of timing, process ownership, and the scope of the certification process.

The people inside the organization then need to be made aware of the plan, and educated as to their role in achieving it.

The journey is not easy, but the benefits are considerable. ISO 9000 forces you into process analysis, and if approached in the right way, can reduce costs by as much as 10 percent. Many large organizations are now making ISO 9000 a prerequisite for doing business, so the cost of not being registered might be higher in the long-term than the 10 percent savings you make.

Remember, the customer is the final arbiter on quality, and in asking you to become registered, they are simply seeking an assurance that your business is being driven in a way that is safe and reliable.

ISO 9000 focuses on your business processes, and is an excellent first step in business process improvement. Keep in mind, though, it is only a basic driver's license, and if you want to be a world class racing driver, you will need to move beyond ISO 9000.

You can use ISO 9000 as a foundation for continuous improvement.

BROWSER'S BRIEFING

- ISO 9000 is a foundation or "starter kit" for an organization's continuous improvement process. It is the international standard for quality assurance.
- If you want to become ISO 9000 registered, your organization will be evaluated by an independent auditor, who will assess whether your organization is "safe to drive" its goods and services in other organizations.
- If your quality system is found reliable, you will be registered and given a certificate, or "driver's license."
- The ISO 9000 standards evolved from the standards originally developed by the British and U.S. military with their suppliers in World War II.
- The requirements you have to meet to be registered to the standard are what most business people would agree are "common sense business practices."
- There are a maximum of 20 requirements to be met if you register to ISO 9001, and 19 for ISO 9002. ISO 9003 has just 16 requirements.
- The customer is the driving force behind ISO 9000.
- The ISO 9000 standards focus on process management, and are involved very little in the "people" issues of quality.
- The whole management team must be involved if a company is to get real benefit from ISO 9000.
- The company must document its quality system, which means writing a policy for each of the business practices to be followed in order to meet the standard.
- A procedure must then be written to show how the policy is carried out.
- If the auditor finds that these policies and practices are a true statement of how you run your business, you will be registered.

21 | Using ISO 9000 to Drive Continuous Improvement

Some time ago, I had a new set of tires put on my car. This is something we've all had done over the years. I went to one of the specialist tire shops, and selected the best buy. They took my tires through to the fitting bay, and raised my car on the ramp. Have you noticed how in every tire bay they follow the same procedure? The mechanic took off all the hubcaps, removed the wheel nuts with the air gun, and then dropped each set of wheel nuts into the appropriate hubcap. The mechanic then took off the left rear wheel, and took it to the machine where he removed the old tire, fitted the new one, and refilled the tire to the correct air pressure.

He then took the newly fitted wheel and tire back to the correct axle on the car, and refitted by hand the nuts he had placed in the hubcap. When the nuts were finger-tight, he used the air gun to tighten them to the correct torque. He then removed the right rear wheel (we're now on the opposite side of the car) and followed the same procedure for replacing the tire. He brought the newly fitted wheel and tire back to the correct axle on the car and replaced by hand the nuts which were, again, waiting in the hubcap.

He then bent down to pick up the air gun, and discovered he'd left it by the first wheel he'd fitted. I could read his mind: "I'll come back to this later!"

So here's my car with one wheel "gun-tight," and the second wheel "finger-tight," and he's moving to do the third wheel. If it were your car, the tension in your stomach would probably be rising like mine was. You'd be thinking, "Will he remember to go back and use the air gun on wheel number two?"

The mechanic had broken the procedure, and the opportunity for error had just increased dramatically. Clearly defining processes and clearly defining procedures is one of your greatest opportunities for improvement in your business, and taking time to do this gives you one of your best returns on the investment of your time. This is the heart of building prevention into your process.

The best discipline for forcing you into developing consistent procedures is ISO 9000. Just think of procedures as a series of subprocesses, and ISO 9000 as a method for forcing you to use the disciplines of process analysis and process management.

By 1995, Britain had registered something like 20,000 companies to the ISO 9000 standards. While the general experience has been good, many thousands of these British companies have allowed ISO 9000 to freeze them into a procedural bureaucracy. What can we learn from their experience? This has usually occurred when the company leaders have not taken the time to understand what ISO 9000 really is, and have not taken a leadership role in managing the change that will occur as a result of establishing a documented quality system, which the standard requires.

Many companies have kept their ISO 9000 initiative quite separate from an existing total quality initiative, recognizing that ISO 9000 is not *total* quality. This has also been a mistake, and has led to duplication of effort and missed opportunity. Total quality involves both process improvement and people improvement, which can typically be broken down into the activities in the model we are now familiar with. ISO 9000 does not concern itself with activities outside the shaded area in Figure 21-1, except for brief passing reference in ISO 9004, which is in any case only an advisory document.

ISO 9000 is concerned with process management, and if we recognize that reality, we can use it to strengthen the process management work in total quality. If we take the trouble to fully understand the requirements of ISO 9000, we can also use it as a foundation for continuous improvement.

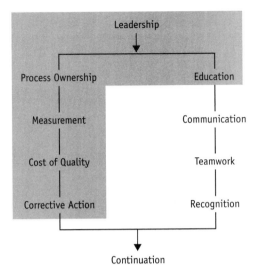

**Figure 21-1. The ISO 9000 Emphasis on
Process Improvement**

IDENTIFYING ISO REQUIREMENTS

The customer is asking, "Do the processes inside this organization that wants to supply me link together in a way that I will get what is promised to me?" So to start with, the organization has to know how its processes link together, and it must know the capability of its internal processes.

ISO has designed a set of requirements which almost any organization can aspire to, and while they have shortcomings, such as excessive wording (the British influence) and the manufacturing bias (the military influence), they do enable an organization to apply a discipline to the way it manages its activities. The most comprehensive standard in the series, ISO 9001, includes the following 20 categories of requirements:

1. Management Responsibility

2. Quality System

3. Contract Review

4. Design Control

5. Document and Data Control

6. Purchasing

7. Control of Customer-Supplied Product

8. Product Identification and Traceability

9. Process Control

10. Inspection and Testing

11. Inspection Equipment

12. Inspection Status

13. Control of Nonconforming Product

14. Corrective and Preventive Action

15. Handling

16. Control of Quality Records

17. Internal Quality Audit

18. Training

19. Servicing

20. Statistical Techniques

Assign a champion for each of the 16, 19, or 20 areas in which you intend to get certified. These people will become the *category owners.*

When you have identified your category owners, each of them needs to set a policy for their category. Take, for example, the third category of contract review. If the vice president of marketing is the category owner, then he or she would write a policy for this process which might read something like Figure 21-2.

Having set this policy, the vice president should show commitment by signing off on the policy, and the other process owners should do the same thing for their processes.

FULFILLING ISO REQUIREMENTS

Having established your policy for each of the 16, 19, or 20 requirements, you now need a method for fulfilling the policy. This draws you into the procedures for fulfilling each policy.

Section 3: Contract Review

3.1: Contracts are reviewed by the marketing department before acceptance for:
- *requirements being clearly defined and documented*
- *lead time required on parts or materials*
- *specific packaging and shipping requirements*

3.2: All necessary departments are consulted as necessary during the contract review.

3.3: Any exceptions to the customer specifications will be agreed to with the customer prior to accepting an order or prior to finalizing a contract.

3.4: Any amendments to an order will be communicated to all persons in the organization who are affected by the change.

Figure 21-2. A Sample Policy for an ISO 9000 Category

We are also suppliers to internal customers, and for the organization's internal linkages to work smoothly, we must agree on requirements with our internal customer. In order to do this, the processes in the business need clear ownership, and one of the first steps you will take in the ISO 9000 journey is to establish clear process ownership.

Once process owners have agreed upon requirements, they can then set about getting the process they own under control and making it predictable. The standard recognizes this by requiring procedures to be defined for each of the processes in the business. The standard also requires the process owner to have the necessary skills to operate the process, and this combined with the right procedure and equipment allows prevention to be built into the process.

Traditionally, people deliver quality to the customer by checking after the fact. Prevention is both cheaper and faster in the long-term. Prevention is the way *we do it right the first time.* Prevention is the way of ensuring we conform to customer requirements *on time, every time.*

However, having established customer requirements and having established processes capable of meeting customer requirements, it is vital that an organization should not become complacent. Your customer will always be looking for you to meet more stringent requirements, and your competitors will always be trying to unseat you from the comfortable relationship with your customer. Continuous improvement of your processes is essential if we are going to continue to delight the customer.

ISO 9000 forces you to analyze your business processes. If you apply the principles of process management, you'll find yourself defining a procedure for each of your key business processes. Remember, procedures are a series of subprocesses for the process you are analyzing, as Figure 21-3 illustrates.

For instance, if you look at contract review, you are asked to define the procedure you follow when you review contracts from your clients. The objective of contract review is to ensure that you are capable of meeting the client's requirements. You simply write down the steps you follow in reviewing contracts:

1. Sales representative receives order by phone or hard copy.

2. Telephone orders are recorded on order desk form.

3. Sales rep checks completion date with operations planner.

4. Pricing is checked with pricing manual.

5. Shipping documents are prepared.

6. Copies of customer orders are filed by customer name.

7. Shipping documents are forwarded to dispatch department.

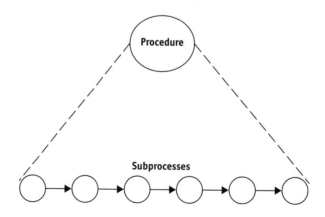

Figure 21-3. Procedures as a Series of Subprocesses

If you realize that Step 3 of checking completion date with your operations planner is something you rarely do, and is often a cause of the problems with your customer, then you have two choices: deal with this nonconformity, or fail to get certification. A great discipline.

THE ORGANIZATION'S PROCESSES

When you look at your own organization's processes, it can be difficult at first sight to relate all of them to the categories of the ISO 9000 standard, but one of the first activities you must conduct is a mapping of your business process flow. ISO 9000 will be a certification of your processes and not your business, so that you must define the boundaries of the process you want to certify.

Recall from Chapter 10 that a simple version of a process flow might look like Figure 21-4. The reality of your business is, of course, far more complicated, and you will notice that I've listed the process owners on the left side of the chart. This mapping activity should be done by the business leaders as a team, and they need to agree on who owns which process. It will be quite an experience of discovery, and I usually find the team unearths a few "orphans"—processes without an owner. A facilitator is often helpful to keep the team on track, and you need to avoid making the map too complicated.

Having defined the scope of the processes in the business you want to certify, you then need to match this to the categories in the standard, using the tool of the matrix.

LINKING "PROCESSES" TO "CATEGORIES"

An example of the matrix is shown in Figure 21-5. The business processes are listed down the left column, and the 20 categories of ISO 9001 are across the top (numbered with the prefix "4" because they are given in section 4 of the standard). Some ISO categories relate to the whole organization, and are shown in the bottom line of the matrix.

This matrixing is the second critical step; it is the interface between the reality of the business and the categories of the standard. Your

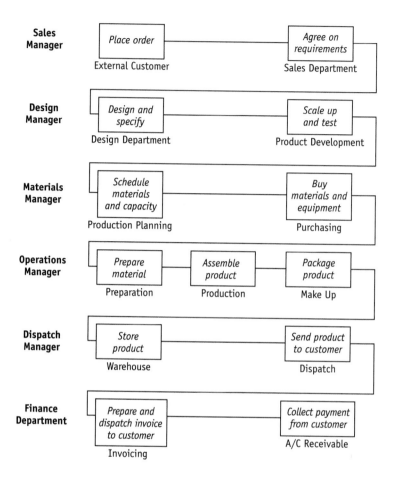

Figure 21-4. A Process Flow Map for a Business Unit

policy manual will state your business objectives and commitment to meeting the 20 categories of the standard, and will be designed around these categories. The procedure manual will describe the procedures followed to execute the processes listed in the left column. Your policy manual will be a brief manual of 20 to 30 pages which, once written, should rarely change. Your procedures manual, on the other hand, should be a living statement of how each of the business processes is carried out.

In the same way that you have established owners for your business processes, you must establish an owner for each of your ISO categories.

	4.1	4.2	4.3	4.4	4.5	4.6	4.7	4.8	4.9	4.10	4.11	4.12	4.13	4.14	4.15	4.16	4.17	4.18	4.19	4.20
Place Order																				
Agree on Requirements			■																	
Design Product				■																
Specify Product				■																
Scale Up				■																
Test										■	■									
Schedule Material									■											
Set Capacity								■	■											
Buy Material						■	■													
Buy Equipment						■														
Prepare Material										■			■	■						
Operations									■	■										
Package													■	■						
Store Product															■					
Dispatch														■	■					
Prepare Invoice																				
Dispatch Invoice																				
Collect Payment																				
All Processes	■	■			■									■		■	■	■	■	■

Figure 21-5. An ISO 9001 Category/Process Matrix

Category	Owner
1. Management Responsibility	President
2. Quality System	VP Quality
3. Contract Review	VP Marketing/Sales
4. Design Control	Chief Engineer/Designer
5. Document and Data Control	VP Quality
6. Purchasing	VP Purchasing
7. Control of Customer-Supplied Product	VP Purchasing
8. Product Identification and Traceability	VP Operations *or* Planning
9. Process Control	VP Operations *and* Planning
10. Inspection and Testing	VP Quality
11. Inspection Equipment	VP Quality
12. Inspection Status	VP Quality
13. Control of Nonconforming Product	VP Operations
14. Corrective and Preventive Action	VP Operations
15. Handling	VP Operations
16. Control of Quality Records	VP Quality
17. Internal Quality Audit	VP Quality
18. Training	VP Human Resources
19. Servicing	VP Marketing/Sales
20. Statistical Methods	VP Manufacturing *or* Quality

Figure 21-6. Suggested Category Owners for ISO 9001

That person will then be responsible for writing the policy statement for their part of the manual. This "ownership" is essential if the management team is to have a stake in the success of the quality system. A list of who might typically be the ISO category owners in a given organization appears as Figure 21-6.

When people talk about quality manuals, they usually talk about the policy manual, and this gets wide exposure in articles and professional publications. So I am going to look more closely at the procedure manual, which is where the action exists (or the bureaucracy, if you're not careful).

THE PROCEDURE MANUAL

If you refer to the matrix in Figure 21-5, you will need to establish procedures for those categories which span the organization (the bottom line of the matrix). These procedures will be relatively simple to define and relate to the "subsystems" of the quality system (e.g., Document Control: Internal Audit). They will link directly to the categories in the policy manual.

Referring back to the business process flowchart in Figure 21-4, there is also a need to establish a procedure for carrying out each process on that chart.

These procedures will need to be cataloged by department, and will relate less directly to the policy manual. Clearly, the person responsible for establishing the departmental procedure is the process owner on that business flowchart.

What the ISO 9000 standards are asking us to do is break down each business level process into departmental processes. Then it suggests analysis to a further level, known as work instructions. This means breaking down a departmental activity into a detailed set of steps. For example, one departmental activity may be raising an invoice. The work instruction consists of the steps involved in raising an invoice.

PROCESS ANALYSIS AND COST OF QUALITY

ISO 9000 is asking you to do process analysis on the business. The analysis should be done by the process owners and subprocess owners, and too many companies lack the courage to do this. They delegate the job to a consultant or to the quality manager, instead of taking the trouble to learn to use the powerful tools of process analysis. The reason most companies lack the courage to carry out process analysis is that they don't realize the potential for financial benefits from process improvement. Cost of quality can show the benefits, and ISO 9004, the guideline document, recommends the use of cost of quality:

> It is important that the effectiveness of a quality system be measured in financial terms. The impact of an effective quality system upon the organization's profit and loss statement can be highly significant, particularly by improvement of operations, resulting in reduced losses due to error and by making a contribution to customer satisfaction.

Notice the word *improvement;* this is not "static" thinking. This sentence means you use cost of quality to select which processes are in most need of attention, and calculate the financial saving from the improvement you make.

Recall the example I gave in Chapter 12 about writing a report for the boss. We found we often unconsciously use cost of waste to improve the way we write this report.

In paragraph 6.3 ISO 9004, the standard says:

The financial reporting of quality activities should be regularly provided to and monitored by management, and be related to other business measures such as "sales," "turnover," or "added value" in order to provide for a realistic, entrepreneurial

- *evaluation of the adequacy and effectiveness of the quality system,*

- *identification of additional areas requiring attention and improvement, and*

- *establishment of quality and cost objectives for the following period.*

What the standard is trying to say is that management should use cost of quality to decide which processes are most in need of improvement, and then set cost and time objectives for this improvement.

We're now starting to see the link to corrective action, and the ISO 9000 corrective action clause is probably the greatest ally of continuous process improvement.

CORRECTIVE ACTION

The Corrective Action clause (4.14) of ISO 9001 reads:

4.14.2—Corrective Action

The procedures for corrective action shall include:

a) *the effective handling of customer complaints and reports of the product non-conformities;*

b) *investigation of the cause of non-conformities relating to product, process and quality system, and recording the results of the investigation (see 4.16);*

c) *determination of the corrective action needed to eliminate the cause of the non-conformities;*

d) *application of controls to ensure that corrective action is taken and that it is effective.*

4.14.3—Preventive Action

The procedures for preventive action shall include:

a) *the use of appropriate sources of information such as process and work operations which affect product quality, concessions, audit results, quality records, service reports and customer complaints to detect, analyze and eliminate potential causes of non-conformities;*

b) *determination of the steps needed to deal with any problems requiring preventive action;*

c) *initiation of preventive action and application of controls to ensure that it is effective;*

d) *confirmation that relevant information on actions taken is submitted for management review;*

e) *initiating preventive actions to deal with problems to a level corresponding with the risks encountered.*

As you read this through, you can see some really key words. Part 14.2 is straightforward; note that it relates to *product.* Most companies investigate the cause of nonconforming products. However, few companies move to part 14.3 in the true spirit of the standard: *"initiation of preventive action."*

We talked about process analysis earlier in this book. This is not process cataloging, which most people do. Process analysis means looking at each procedure that you map, and then redesigning it (the fashionable word is reengineer!) to ensure it is always capable of delivering what is promised.

Weak procedures provide opportunity for error (e.g., where you rely on someone's memory).

Part 14.3 of the corrective action clause shows the linkage to cost of quality, which we discussed earlier: *"initiating preventive actions to deal with problems to a level corresponding with the risks encountered."*

This means you have to prioritize the problems you work on, and you do this on the basis of cost.

Notice also in the requirements the words *potential* and *preventive*. The standard is not satisfied with a reactive mode, and the 1994 ISO 9000 revision has strengthened the wording here.

In 14.2d, the words *"application of controls to ensure that corrective action is... effective"* mean that a corrective action system must be a key part of the process improvement activity. This ensures revisiting the processes and continuously improving them, based on cost of quality information. The flowchart of a typical corrective action system is shown in Figure 21-7, and was detailed more fully in Chapter 13.

With this approach, you can make ISO 9000 a foundation for continuous improvement.

Corrective Action System Flow

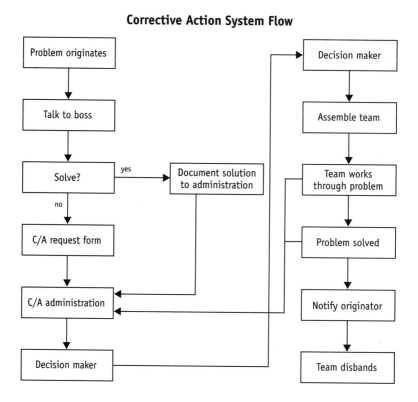

Figure 21-7. Flowchart for a Corrective Action System

BROWSER'S BRIEFING

- Leadership must own the ISO 9000 qualification process if it is to produce benefits for the organization.
- ISO 9000 is only "partial" quality, and does not get involved with the "people" issues of total quality.
- ISO 9000 is based on process management.
- A business is structured differently from the standard, and the processes of a business must be matrixed with the requirements of the standard.
- The business processes and also the requirements of the standard must be given clear "owners."
- Development of the procedure manual offers an opportunity to improve and reengineer business processes.
- Using a cost of quality assessment to evaluate business processes enables an organization to be selective in where it applies its finite resources for corrective action.
- The ISO 9000 standard requires a company to have a corrective action system.
- Simply cataloging business procedures deprives you of a great opportunity for business improvement.

22 | The New Organization

In the last 1,000 years we have seen the widespread development of urban civilization. In the last 100 years, the modern business organization has developed, and its models have been the organizations of government and the military. Over the last millennium, government organizations were developed to retain the status quo and not respond to change. Military structure relied on death in battle as a way of ensuring new opportunities for the survivors.

In the past decade, North America has woken up to the need to redesign the business organization as we have known it.

At the start of this book, we talked about the vision of the organization. As you worked through each of the things you must do, you almost unconsciously developed your own picture of what your organization should look like. You probably see that now we are looping back to the "Vision" chapter at the start of this process, but with much more concrete ideas than when we did it the first time. The word *continuous* has developed even greater meaning.

You have to build continuation into your process, or it will just become a one-shot project that fades into obscurity.

Philip Crosby and James Belasco both talk about celebration of the passing of the old ways and the welcoming of the new as reinforcing the "move forward" or "rite of passage" that has occurred. Organizations find that after 18 to 24 months the enthusiasm can fade, or at some point a major event, such as a CEO change or a change in business direction, can leave the quality process out on a limb. This underlines the importance of integrating the quality plan with the business plan.

The new culture of the organization, the new way of doing things, the changes that have occurred since the start of the process; all of these things need to be identified, and the differences from the old culture and methods need to be clearly shown.

The most successful way of doing this is by celebrating the change. Philip Crosby calls it "Zero Defects Day." Organizations have used different names, like "Milestone Day," or "Hearts and Minds Day."

A self-assessment along the lines of the Baldrige criteria at the beginning of the process and every six to nine months afterward will tell you how far you have actually progressed.

What are the things you expect to have changed when you successfully run through The Wall of the Quality Marathon?

THE NEW VISION

You will be much clearer who your customers are, and what they need from you. Everyone in the organization will understand who their internal and external customers are, and will realize their success will only come when these customers are happy. Negative customer feedback will be seen as an opportunity, and won't be dismissed or argued away as some special case that won't recur.

You ever-developing vision will be shared by all the people in the organization. Everyone will at some time in the year be looking at another organization either on video or in person, and benchmarking against other best practices. Books and cassette tapes will reinforce the knowledge people have about what your organization should look like.

You will be able to define your culture, and have a clear sense of what the values are inside your organization. You will recruit people whose values are your values. Your people will strive to understand their customers' requirements, and will insist on operating processes that do it right the first time. They will always look for new ways to improve themselves and their processes. You will understand how your culture compares with that of your community and your nation. A statement of those values will be built into your quality policy, which people will take as a simple fact of life.

Change will be welcomed, and everyone will be a participant in change. People won't change people; people will change themselves, because of the desire to do things faster, simpler, and better. Your organization will invest a significant proportion of its time in change and improvement.

Your change process will be well-defined, and you will be measuring success in each aspect of this process. Everyone will understand that the balance of people and process (hard skills) is essential for continuous improvement, and the process will have been shared with everyone in the organization. The management team will review progress in the quality process every month, and the QMT decisions will be deployed rapidly into the appropriate parts of the organization by the team member who represents that part. People will feel empowered, and quality champions who are not business leaders will have become members of the QMT. This will not have been forced; it will be a natural development.

The leaders of the organization will participate in the quality process every bit as much as the rest of the people. The leaders will routinely measure processes they personally own in order to improve the delivery they give to their internal customer, and their measurement efforts will be visible to all. The self-esteem of the organization will be high, as will the self-esteem of the individuals and especially the leaders. The consequence is that the leaders will be open and honest. They will be certainly improving their skills.

Your business processes will have been mapped, and you will have mapped at each department level. Each individual will be clear on their responsibilities, and will know who are their internal and external customers, and what the requirements are of those customers. After two years, most people will have worked on five or six process problems with their internal customers, and arrived at successful conclusions. You will have reengineered many of your process flows, and cut out excessive communication in your organization.

Measurement will have become an integral part of the culture. It will be used at all external customer interfaces, and "measurement partnerships" with external customers will drive business process improvement. The interdepartmental measures (the second level of measurement) will show teams how well they deliver to the next team in the chain, and individuals within those teams will measure their personal processes which contribute to the team process. The tools of measurement will be understood by everyone, and the measurement successes will be on record. SPC will have been used at certain technical points in the organization, but you will be ready to move it to much wider usage.

All of this measurement data will be fed into your continuous cost of quality collection, and you will show reductions in cost of quality which will be three, five, or ten times the investment you have made in the quality process. Cost of quality will be understood as widely as measurement, and you will use it routinely to communicate the effects of nonconformance.

The cost of quality system will feed the corrective action system, and you will have cross-functional teams, which will be increased from the five or six teams two years ago to a number which includes every employee in the organization. The corrective action system will also be driven by external customer issues, and your external customers will all know how to raise a nonconformance issue within your organization.

You will be very clear that your investment in education and training will be one of the best investments you can make in your people and your organization, and everyone in the organization will be hungry for the next piece of knowledge they are going to acquire. This will be skills and knowledge about their processes, and about improving their processes. Team leaders will have become coaches, constantly seeking to improve their coaching skills.

Among the skills the people will have developed will be their communication abilities. They will be able to communicate with each other more effectively because of the increased trust and respect between each other. You will probably still be investing in development of people's communication skills and investing in communication technology, but being careful not to eliminate interpersonal contact. You will be much more careful about avoiding information overload, and your organization will have developed an effective internal communication system for team briefing.

The relationship between people in the organization will have changed to a point where the mutual trust and respect will have increased, so teams operate on a very different basis.

The trust and respect will show itself in the way people recognize the achievements of others. Both the organization and the individuals within it will have a high self-esteem and people will not feel threatened by the success of others. They will see the success of others as contributing to the greater good of everyone and recognition will be both systematic in the organization and spontaneous between individuals.

The quality journey will be continuous and people will always be looking for a better way to operate their business processes and a better way to operate the quality improvement process. Benchmarking partners will drive the organization to seek ever better ways of doing this. Regular assessment of the quality process and business processes and comparison with the benchmark partners will drive continuous improvement.

Above all, everyone in the organization will have taken personal responsibility for making quality happen and will assume that responsibility as a member of a team and not as an individual.

SO WHAT DO WE DO NOW?

One of the biggest reasons organizations have failed to do it right the first time is that everyone thought someone else would do it.

Reading this book isn't "doing it." Until you and everyone you work with individually and together accept that *you* must move forward, then it won't happen.

The passion and commitment is essential. The measurement and analysis is essential. The two sides of the quality brain must ultimately blend, and when that happens it may be hard for you to describe to others what has happened. The effect will be exciting, and you will find yourself ever hungry for knowledge and forever wishing to share your revelations with others. You will applaud excellent service and speak out against organizations who abuse your custom.

I am writing this last chapter on a unique day in my life. It is my birthday and I am alone for the first time in my life on my birthday, and I am probably in the last place I would have chosen to be. I arrived in Las Vegas last night to attend the ASQC Annual Quality Congress that starts tomorrow. In my short stay here, Las Vegas has presented me with a microcosm of the world of quality.

I am staying at one of two hotels in the city owned by a prominent name in the hospitality industry. This company's name has always meant "the best" throughout my life, and one of the two hotels here lives up to that name. Sadly the one where I am staying has demonstrated a number of the failings of a decaying corporation. The frontline staff protest, "I am only doing my job," and blame outside organizations and influences for their problems. They clearly have no sense of belonging to their hotel.

In my first 24 hours in the hotel I had to wait 30 minutes to check in, I was unable to make two critical international phone calls because the front desk did not process my registration correctly, and I came close to missing my evening meal reservation because the valet service took 15 minutes to deliver my automobile.

The counterpoint to this experience was a restaurant on Sixth Street South, Andre Rochat's, which has all the attributes of the Maistrali restaurant in Crete described in Chapter 2. Rochat's establishment provides an outstanding product—about the best you will ever eat—but even more important, the service is impeccable. The people in the restaurant work as a team and Andre leads the team. They have the technical stuff worked out and they also have the people stuff worked out.

Las Vegas is a boom town. It's like the United States in the 1950s. You don't need to worry about the customer when business is good. If your own organization emerges from a tough business situation and customers become easier to find because of the economy, remember that it's during the good times that you will make the friends who will help you survive the cycle of bad times.

I wrote to the general manager of the hotel I stayed at. I spoke to the front desk manager and explained my bad experiences. I spoke to Andre and each of his staff and complimented them on the excellent food and service they provided. It is essential to tell your suppliers when they have succeeded or failed in meeting your requirements. Equally, when our own customers give us feedback we must learn to welcome the information and see it as an opportunity for improvement. It is too easy to be defensive and justify our own nonconformances.

This is part of the personal side of quality. The other side of the coin is that we must clearly start to work on our own day-to-day activities.

How do we start to build quality in our own work processes? I find that people who first get into quality want to know more about time management. Intuitively they sense that time management is really self-management, and that the starting point for any quality journey is always with yourself.

All of what we have talked about in this book applies to us as individuals; we can apply the principles of leadership, process improvement, and personal improvement to our own lives. You'll find it works far more quickly and easily if you share the experiences in a "buddy" system, better still if you share with the team you work with, and best of all if you share with your organization as a whole.

The first step is self-management and the recognition that in the last analysis, we are ourselves responsible for the results of our own actions.

BROWSER'S BRIEFING

- Celebrating the passing of the old organization is essential.
- The quality plan and the business plan must become one and the same.
- The difference between the new and the old organization must be clearly shown.
- Overlooking this rite of passage will cause you to "hit The Wall" in your change process after about 18 months.
- You must build the physical and psychological momentum to run through this wall.
- To do this, you will have to have a clear vision of the quality organization you want to be.
- Your values and your culture will be clearly defined.
- Your people will work for the customer, and not for a supervisor.
- Change will be welcomed, and you will be measuring the effectiveness of your own change process, which will have a balance of process improvement and people improvement.
- The leaders and the people will have a high sense of self-worth and will be open and honest with each other.
- The business process will be clearly defined, and measurement will have become an integral part of the culture.
- You will benchmark with other successful companies, and you will be an outward-looking organization.
- You will communicate with your suppliers as enthusiastically as with your customers.
- You will recognize that quality management is about success, and success comes from self-management.
- You will recognize we are responsible for our own successes, which are the result of our own actions.

References

Bowles, Jerry, and Joshua Hammond. *Beyond Quality.* New York: Putnam, 1991.

Clemmer, Jim, with Barry Sheehy. *Firing on All Cylinders: The Service/Quality System for High-Powered Corporate Performance.* Homewood, IL: Business One Irwin, 1992.

Crosby, Philip B. *Quality Without Tears.* New York, McGraw-Hill, 1984.

de Bono, Edward W. *Sur Petition (Going Beyond Competition): Creating Value Monopolies When Everyone Else Is Merely Competing.* New York: Harper Business, 1993.

Juran, J.M. *Juran on Leadership for Quality: An Executive Handbook.* New York: Free Press, 1989.

Kouzes, James M., and Barry Z. Posner. *The Leadership Challenge: How to Get Extraordinary Things Done in Organizations,* 2nd edition. San Francisco: Jossey-Bass, 1995.

Laborde, Genie Z. *Influencing with Integrity: Management Skills for Communication and Negotiation.* Palo Alto: Syntony Publishing, 1983.

National Institute of Standards and Technology, U.S. Department of Commerce. *Malcolm Baldrige National Quality Award: Criteria for Performance Excellence,* 1997.

Senge, Peter M. *The Fifth Discipline: Mastering the Five Practices of the Learning Organization.* New York: Doubleday, 1992.

Watson, Jr., Thomas J. *A Business and Its Beliefs: The Ideas That Helped Build IBM.* New York: McGraw-Hill, 1963.

About the Author

Peter Merrill was born and educated in the U.K. and graduated from Birmingham University as a chemical engineer. He has over 30 years of business experience, including 20 years with the Courtaulds Corporation. He rose to the position of chief executive of one of the businesses in that corporation, doubling the size of the business in two years and putting into practice a quality improvement process.

In 1987 Merrill joined Philip Crosby Associates as a vice president, and initiated the implementation of quality improvement in both North America and Europe. He is now president of Strider International, a consulting firm specializing in implementation of quality improvement and ISO 9000 implementation.

Merrill is a frequent speaker at quality conferences, a member of the Canadian national committee on ISO 9000, past chairman of the Toronto chapter of the American Society for Quality Control, and a member of the advisory board at Ryerson University Business School. His leisure activities are varied, including rugby, golf, and skiing, and he enjoys painting and a wide variety of music.

Index

Books from Productivity Press

Productivity Press publishes books that empower individuals and companies to achieve excellence in quality, productivity, and the creative involvement of all employees. Through steadfast efforts to support the vision and strategy of continuous improvement, Productivity Press delivers today's leading-edge tools and techniques gathered directly from industry leaders around the world. Call toll-free (800)394-6868 for our free catalog.

20 Keys to Workplace Improvement (Revised Edition)
Iwao Kobayashi
The 20 Keys system does more than just bring together twenty of the world's top manufacturing improvement approaches—it integrates these individual methods into a closely interrelated system for revolutionizing every aspect of your manufacturing organization. This revised edition of Kobayashi's bestseller amplifies the synergistic power of raising the levels of all these critical areas simultaneously. The new edition presents upgraded criteria for the five-level scoring system in most of the 20 Keys, supporting your progress toward becoming not only best in your industry but best in the world.
ISBN 1-56327-109-5/ 302 pages / $50.00 / Order 20KREV-B275

Achieving Total Quality Management
A Program for Action
Michel Perigord
This is an outstanding book on total quality management (TQM)—a compact guide to the concepts, methods, and techniques involved in achieving total quality. It shows you how to make TQM a companywide strategy, not just in technical areas, but in marketing and administration as well. Written in an accessible, instructive style by a top European quality expert, it is methodical, logical, and thorough. Major methods and tools for total quality are spelled out and implementation strategies are reviewed.
ISBN 0-915299-60-7 / 392 pages / $50.00 / Order ACHTQM-B275

Building a Shared Vision
A Leader's Guide to Aligning the Organization
C. Patrick Lewis
This exciting new book presents a step-by-step method for developing your organizational vision. It teaches how to build and maintain a shared vision directed from the top down, but encompassing the views of all the members and stakeholders, and understanding the competitive environment of the organization. Like *Corporate Diagnosis,* this books describes in detail one of the necessary first steps from *Implementing a Lean Management System:* visioning.
ISBN 1-56327-163-X / 150 pages / $45.00 / Order VISION-B275

Caught in the Middle
A Leadership Guide for Partnership in the Workplace
Rick Maurer
Managers today are caught between old skills and new expectations. You're expected not only to improve quality and services, but also to get staff more involved. This stimulating book provides the inspiration and know-how to achieve these goals as it brings to light the rewards of establishing a real partnership with your staff. Includes self-assessment questionnaires.
ISBN 1-56327-158-3 / 258 pages / $30.00 / Order CAUGHT-B275

Companywide Quality Management
Alberto Galgano
Companywide quality management (CWQM) leads to dramatic changes in management values and priorities, company culture, management of company operations, management and decision-making processes, techniques and methods used by employees, and more. Much has been written on this subject, but Galgano—a leading European consultant who studied with leaders of the Japanese quality movement—offers hands-on, stage-front knowledge of the monumental changes CWQC can bring.
ISBN 1-56327-038-2 / 480 pages / $45.00 / Order CWQM-B275

Corporate Diagnosis
Setting the Global Standard for Excellence
Thomas L. Jackson with Constance E. Dyer

All too often, strategic planning neglects an essential first step and final step-diagnosis of the organization's current state. What's required is a systematic review of the critical factors in organizational learning and growth, factors that require monitoring, measurement, and management to ensure that your company competes successfully. This executive workbook provides a step-by-step method for diagnosing an organization's strategic health and measuring its overall competitiveness against world class standards. With checklists, charts, and detailed explanations, *Corporate Diagnosis* is a practical instruction manual. The pillars of Jackson's diagnostic system are strategy, structure, and capability. Detailed diagnostic questions in each area are provided as guidelines for developing your own self-assessment survey.

ISBN 1-56327-086-2 / 115 pages / $65.00 / Order CDIAG-B275

Fast Focus on TQM
A Concise Guide to Companywide Learning
Derm Barrett

Finally, here's one source for all your TQM questions. Compiled in this concise, easy-to-read handbook are definitions and detailed explanations of over 160 key terms used in TQM. Organized in a simple alphabetical glossary form, the book can be used either as a primer for anyone being introduced to TQM or as a complete reference guide. It helps to align teams, departments, or entire organizations in a common understanding and use of TQM terminology. For anyone entering or currently involved in TQM, this is one resource you must have.

ISBN 1-56327-049-8 / 205 pages / $20.00 / Order FAST-B275

Feedback Toolkit
16 Tools for Better Communication in the Workplace
Rick Maurer

In companies striving to reduce hierarchy and foster trust and responsible participation, good person-to-person feedback can be as important as sophisticated computer technology in enabling effective teamwork.

Feedback is an important map of your situation, a way to tell whether you are "on or off track." Used well, feedback can motivate people to their highest level of performance. Despite its significance, this level of information sharing makes most managers uncomfortable. *Feedback Toolkit* addresses this natural hesitation with an easy-to-grasp 6-step framework and 16 practical and creative approaches for giving and receiving feedback with individuals and groups.

ISBN 1-56327-056-0 / 109 pages / $12.00 / Order FEED-B275

Handbook of Quality Tools
The Japanese Approach
Tetsuichi Asaka and Kazuo Ozeki (eds.)
The Japanese have stunned the world by their ability to produce top quality products at competitive prices. This comprehensive teaching manual, which includes the seven traditional and five newer QC tools, explains each tool, why it's useful, and how to construct and use it. It's a perfect training aid, as well as a hands-on reference book, for supervisors, foremen, and/or team leaders. Accessible to everyone in your organization, dealing with both management and shop floor how-to's, you'll find it an indispensable tool in your quest for quality. Information is presented in easy-to-grasp language, with step-by-step instructions, illustrations, and examples of each tool.

ISBN 1-56327-138-9 / 315 pages / $30.00 / Order HQTP-B275

Implementing a Lean Management System
Thomas L. Jackson with Karen R. Jones
Does your company think and act ahead of technological change, ahead of the customer, and ahead of the competition? Thinking strategically requires a company to face these questions with a clear future image of itself. *Implementing a Lean Management System* lays out a comprehensive management system for aligning the firm's vision of the future with market realities. Based on hoshin management, the Japanese strategic planning method used by top managers for driving TQM throughout an organization, *Lean Management* is about deploying vision, strategy, and policy to all levels of daily activity. It is an eminently practical methodology emerging out of the implementation of continuous improvement

methods and employee involvement. The key tools of this book build on multiskilling, the knowledge of the worker, and an understanding of the role of the new lean manufacturer.
ISBN 1-56327-085-4 / 182 pages / $65.00 / Order ILMS-B275

The Improvement Engine
Creativity and Innovation Through Employee Involvement: The Kaizen Teian System
JHRA (ed.)

The Improvement Engine offers the most all inclusive information available today on this proven method for increasing employee involvement. Kaizen Teian is a technique developed in Japan for encouraging employees to constantly look for and make improvement suggestions. This book explores the subtleties between designing a moderately successful program and a highly successful one and includes a host of tools, techniques, and case studies.
ISBN 1-56327-010-2 / 195 pages / $40.00 / Order IMPENG-B275

ISO 9000 REQUIRED
Your Worldwide Passport to Customer Confidence
Branimir Todorov

ISO 9000 certification is the required passport for suppliers who want to do global business today, and this book tells what you must do to qualify for it. Much has been written about implementation of ISO 9000, from detailed handbooks to full-length works focusing on a single aspect such as documentation Branimir Todorov's *ISO 9000 Required* fills the need for a compact and readable guide for managers to the basics of ISO. Avoiding confusing and unnecessary details, the book is a valuable primer for managers looking for a basic introduction to the ISO standards, as well as an accessible reference to key topics fro readers already involved in ISO certification.
ISBN 1-56327-112-5 / 224 pages, illustrated / $27.00 /
Order ISOREQ-B275

Learning Organizations
Developing Cultures for Tomorrow's Workplace
Sarita Chawla and John Renesch, Editors
The ability to learn faster than your competition may be the only sustainable competitive advantage! A learning organization is one where people continually expand their capacity to create results they truly desire, where new and expansive patterns of thinking are nurtured, where collective aspiration is set free, and where people are continually learning how to learn together. This compilation of 34 powerful essays, written by recognized experts worldwide, is rich in concept and theory as well as application and example. An inspiring follow-up to Peter Senge's groundbreaking bestseller *The Fifth Discipline.*
ISBN 1-56327-110-9 / 571 pages / $35.00 / Order LEARN-B275

A New American TQM
Four Practical Revolutions in Management
Shoji Shiba, Alan Graham, and David Walden
For TQM to succeed in America, you need to create an American-style "learning organization" with the full commitment and understanding of senior managers and executives. Written expressly for this audience, *A New American TQM* offers a comprehensive and detailed explanation of TQM and how to implement it, based on courses taught at MIT's Sloan School of Management and the Center for Quality Management, a consortium of American companies. Full of case studies and amply illustrated, the book examines major quality tools and how they are being used by the most progressive American companies today.
ISBN 1-56327-032-3 / 598 pages / $50.00 / Order NATQM-B275

Secrets of a Successful Employee Recognition System
Daniel C. Boyle
As the human resource manager of a failing manufacturing plant, Dan Boyle was desperate to find a way to motivate employees and break down the barrier between management and the union. He came up with a simple idea to say thank you to your employees for doing their job. In *Secrets of a Successful Employee Recognition System*, Boyle outlines how to begin and run a 100 Club program. Filled with case studies and

detailed guidelines, this book underscores the power behind thanking your employees for a job well done.
ISBN 1-56327-083-8 / 250 pages / $25.00 / Order SECRET-B275

Stepping Up to ISO 14000
Integrating Environmental Quality with ISO 9000 and TQM
Subhash C. Puri

The newest ISO standards, announced in mid-1996, require environmentally-friendly practices in every aspect of a manufacturing business, from factory design and raw material acquisition to the production, packaging, distribution, and ultimate disposal of the product. Here's a comprehensible overview and implementation guide to the standards that's also the only one to show how they fit with current ISO 9000 efforts and other companywide programs for Total Quality Management (TQM).
ISBN 1-56327-129-X / 280 pages / $39.00 / Order STPISO-B275

The Unshackled Organization
Facing the Challenge of Unpredictability Through Spontaneous Reorganization
Jeffrey Goldstein

Managers should not necessarily try to solve all the internal problems within their organizations; intervention may help in the short term, but in the long run may inhibit true problem-solving change from taking place. And change is the real goal. Through change comes real hope for improvement. Using leading-edge scientific and social theories about change, Goldstein explores how change happens within an organization and reveals that only through "self-organization" can natural, lasting change occur. This book is a pragmatic guide for managers, executives, consultants, and other change agents.
ISBN 1-56327-048-X / 202 pages / $25.00 / Order UO-B275

TO ORDER: Write, phone, or fax Productivity Press, Dept. BK, P.O. Box 13390, Portland, OR 97213-0390, phone 1-800-394-6868, fax 1-800-394-6286.

Outside the U.S. phone (503) 235-0600; fax (503) 235-0909

Send check or charge to your credit card (American Express, Visa, MasterCard accepted).

U.S. ORDERS: Add $5 shipping for first book, $2 each additional for UPS surface delivery. Add $5 for each AV program containing 1 or 2 tapes; add $12 for each AV program containing 3 or more tapes. We offer attractive quantity discounts for bulk purchases of individual titles; call for more information.

ORDER BY E-MAIL: Order 24 hours a day from anywhere in the world. Use either address:

To order: **service@ppress.com**
To view the online catalog and/or order: **http://www.ppress.com/**

QUANTITY DISCOUNTS: For information on quantity discounts, please contact our sales department.

INTERNATIONAL ORDERS: Write, phone, or fax for quote and indicate shipping method desired. For international callers, telephone number is 503-235-0600 and fax number is 503-235-0909. Prepayment in U.S. dollars must accompany your order (checks must be drawn on U.S. banks). When quote is returned with payment, your order will be shipped promptly by the method requested.

NOTE: Prices are in U.S. dollars and are subject to change without notice.